To Mom, She has always been there for me and always will be.

Prologue

I WAS DRIVING ON A ROAD THAT, ACCORDING TO *USA Today*, has the most breathtaking scenery and is the most beautiful place to live in America. It is the road from Sedona, Arizona, to a neighboring town, the Village of Oak Creek. I sped along on the newly refurbished highway, enjoying the magnificent countryside. The sun was beginning to set. It was after 7 p. m., in the middle of July. The red rocks looked their best at this time of day. The setting sun brought out the warmth in the rust colored peaks and spires that dominate the landscape.

I was looking forward to attending a birthday party. There would be a great meal and great friends waiting for me at the end of the drive. It was the birthday party for a medical intuitive named Kibira. She was going to be 65 the next day. I didn't know her that well, but I enjoyed being in the company of our mutual friends. It felt good to be surrounded by people like myself: psychics, mediums and healers. Sedona, Arizona is known as one of the New Age centers of the world. That is why I love living here; I can be myself and be around people that accept me and the talents that I have developed over the years.

When I passed through the front door of the house where the party was now in progress, I noticed that the group of about 15 people were all sitting in the living room chatting. I pulled up a chair and sat down, eager to find out what the group was discussing. With these people, the conversation could be anything from UFOs to Brazilian psychic surgeons. As I started to tune into the conversation, I heard a familiar name come up: Ian Xel Lungold.

It was not unusual for him to be the topic of conversation. He had just died a tormented death the previous Thanksgiving. It had been very public. His decline had been documented on the Internet. I had more information about Ian than anyone else in the group. I had lived and worked with him for two years. I had been a part of an important time in his life.

A few minutes after I started talking to the group the room was quiet. Everyone was listening to me. I started to share what I knew about Ian and our connection to Mayan calendar astrology. I was surprised at the interest of the group. I had disassociated myself from Ian after we parted ways, five years earlier. Our relationship had been the most euphoric and harrowing of any I had ever experienced. Even so, I did have a lot to say. I started to answer some of the questions that the group had about Ian when the hostess called us to dinner.

After a great buffet of delicious food, we all sat around the large dining room table and started the happy birthday ritual: the presents, the song, and finally the cake. We were all oohing and ahing about the cake, when Ian's name came up again. I wondered why everyone was still thinking about him. Then I felt all eyes on me again. I took my cue from the group and I continued my story about Ian where I left off. After speaking for a few moments, I started to feel what could only be described as a heaviness filling the room. As I spoke, the atmosphere in the room was beginning to feel a bit creepy to me.

Everyone felt the energy in the room. Alana, who specialized in being a medium, started
to speak.

"Ian is here. He wants you to write his story," she said softly.

Everyone agreed that it felt like we were at a séance. I sensed that he was listening, with glee, to all the interest in his work on the astrology of the Maya and their calculations of the cycles of the universe. I shrugged my shoulders, nodded my head and said, "Yes, I should. It is an incredible story." We all tried to shift the conversation, but the heaviness in the room would not go away. I could not do anything but talk about Ian. Everyone else could do nothing but listen.

We were all feeling a bit weird, so we all got up and started to leave. Poor Kibirah, Ian had stolen the spotlight on her birthday—even from the grave! I knew she didn't mind. I had not seen her for a while. She did not look well and I felt that she would be joining him soon. That happened the following year.

As I got back onto the highway to go back to Sedona, I decided to have a talk with Ian. He was hanging around, so why not? I was yelling at Ian on the entire 25-minute drive back to my house.

"OK, Ian. So you want me to write your story? Well, I need a new computer. I need a laptop." I was probably the only person on the planet in 2006 who did not have a laptop. "And I do not want just any old computer. I want a top of the line, brand new laptop. I want one with all the latest gadgets." I didn't really know what those gadgets were, but I wanted them. I kept yelling at the roof of my car. "And I want it now!" This went on all the way home. It felt good to roar at him. It had taken me a long time to get over the ordeal that my time with Ian had bestowed upon me. That night was uneventful. No midnight messages, no bumps in the night, which I had often experienced when the dead want to chit-chat.

I STARTED WORKING AROUND THE HOUSE THE NEXT morning. It was the usual: clean the cat box, make the bed, etc. Around noon that day, I decided to take a break and have some lunch. I turned on the Travel Channel to keep me company. I like to see all the places in the world that I haven't visited. I have the hope that by looking at them, I will someday be able to go there.

While I was munching on some leftover German potato salad from the night before, an ad came on the Travel Channel for another cable station, QVC, a home shopping network. The ad was talking about a computer sale, which was going to start in half an hour.

"WOW," was all I could say. "Ian, you Sneak! You want me to get this computer, don't you!" I am glad I didn't hear an answer, but I knew the answer was yes.

It turned out that the computer I was able to buy was the latest model, with all the latest gadgets. I was able to make four payments, that all fit into my life plan. Overnight, I had a great computer.

"Oh, my god! Now I actually have to write our story!" It would be three years, almost exactly to the date I got the computer, before I was able to write this story. I was given a message that I could not ignore in May of 2009. It was time for me to write the story of my experiences with Ian.

WHEN I FIRST MET IAN, I SAW SOMETHING THAT I HAD never seen before around a person's head. I saw lightning bolts. All around his head were long, narrow, grey lightning bolts. They formed a crescent around his head and neck. Later I learned that the Maya called this body lightning. The Maya considered the body lightning to be a gift from the Mayan gods. It came through for people born into certain Mayan astrological signs. Ian was one such astrology sign. The body lightning manifests at a ceremony or in this case, an important meeting. I know now that witnessing the body lightning was a sign that we had a special connection. It was an announcement of many extraordinary things to come.

Ian had come to a free lecture that I had given about a meditation class I was scheduled to teach. A friend of his brought him. Ian had a strong interest in what has been called sacred geometry. That was the basis of my workshop.

Ian was a tall, slender man, bordering on skinny. He had long, dark brown hair that spiraled down to his shoulders in tight, corkscrew curls. His eyes were light blue. He had a mustache and a short beard. He was wearing a white shirt, called a Mexican wedding shirt that I had seen many times when I traveled to Southern Mexico.

When I saw the lightning bolts form a crescent around his head, I also felt a jolt of energy. I could not help but think that there was something out of the ordinary about this man. He did stand out, even without the body lightning. He was a handsome, striking man and I felt attracted to him. He emitted a blend of charisma and mystery that was very appealing.

After all the interested people had given me deposits and had left, he was still there. He wanted to attend my workshop but did not have the funds. He had been working on the astrology component of the Mayan calendar. A new method for discovering one's Mayan astrology sign had come to him. He had applied his method to the work of a woman who called herself Luna Bliss.

Ian woefully, and with great panache, told me his financial story. He was dedicating himself to Mayan astrology. He was sure that his projects would yield him and all that had helped him great financial prosperity. He was living in a room of a friend's house and selling Luna's Mayan astrology books to pay for his rent. In a few months, he would speak with Mayan elders and show them his work. He wanted the approval of his invention from the Mayan Council of Elders. With this approval, he felt that he could sell his invention and become exceedingly prosperous.

I wanted to help everyone who was interested in the workshop to receive the knowledge. He was very interested! I wanted to see more of him, and the workshop was the perfect way to get to know him.

THE FIRST DAY OF THE WORKSHOP CAME QUICKLY. AS the participants started to enter the house, I found myself eagerly looking for Ian. He arrived late and sat a distance from the others.

He talked to me a great deal during all the breaks. He was able to reiterate all the information, so I felt he was getting a good grasp of the knowledge. He also practiced the meditation technique with great zeal. He was very sincere when it came to learning the meditation. It was an ascension meditation created by a man called Drunvalo Melchizedek. Its purpose is to assist one in traveling to higher realms of consciousness when a physical pole shift would occur on the earth. In the workshop, it is mentioned that a pole shift has happened many times on the earth. The meditation was designed to take you safely through the days of darkness when the poles shifted and mankind attained a new level of consciousness.

As the workshop was coming to an end, I got a surprise from Ian. He asked me if I could do some massage on his back. I had talked about myself during the free lecture. One of the money-making talents I have become skilled at over the years is massage therapy. He said he was experiencing a great deal of pain. He went on to tell me the story of how he had hurt his back and that often he could not stand up.

I could see there was a problem when he walked. He also made it clear that the massage work would be a trade. He said he would give me some of his jewelry for my work. Did I care what he paid me? Hell, no! I just wanted to see him again.

A FEW NIGHTS LATER, I WENT TO THE HOUSE WHERE HE was staying in Gilbert, AZ. I walked into his room and saw a room unlike any I had ever seen. I was amazed, scared and totally captivated. It gave the overall impression of being an Arabic tent. It had many colors and types of material all overlapping each other. I found the tent very exotic and creative. It had bits of lace, calico, stripes, prints and other designs in the materials that were draped across the ceiling and down the walls. The lighting was very soft with many candles burning. When I walked into the room, I definitely felt that I was walking into a different time. It was very sensual. He told me it was his pirate tent and that he felt he had been a pirate in a past life. I appreciated the originality of the room.

That night, before we got to the massage, he brought me up to speed about what was important to him. It was on that night that he introduced me to Mayan astrology. He told me that the Maya had a very extraordinary system of astrology. The astrology calendar was one of several calendars of the Maya. It was distinctive from any other ancient method of astrology, such as the Hindu or Chinese astrology. This system of astrology has three goals: to help you define who you are, to understand and interact harmoniously with others and assist you to use the energy of each day in a way that is best for you. It was a very simple system to follow. In the time of the ancient Maya, everyone knew what day to do ceremony, what day to do business, what day was good to travel, etc. Their astrology helped the Maya to be a productive and harmonious civilization.

The primary element of the Mayan astrological system is the day lord. The day lord is equivalent to our sun signs, like Libra and Gemini. The Mayan astrology signs are called day lords because they represent the energies that influence the upper world andthe conscious minds of humans. The Lords of Night rule the underworld, where all the riches of the planet reside as well as the energy that is within the subconscious storehouse of the human mind. However, there are 20 day lords in Mayan astrology instead of the familiar 12 sun signs of Gregorian or Western astrology. The astrology that most of us are familiar with is based on the Gregorian calendar.

In addition to the day lord or sun sign, a number from one to thirteen is combined with the day lord. The number six represents flow. The number nine represents patience, etc. Together, the day lord and number give you the essence of who you are. If your day lord is Dog, then you are loyal, warm hearted, intelligent and you love to travel. If you are a 9 Dog, then you are also patient and complete projects.

In addition to helping you find out more about yourself and people with whom you interact, there is another facet to Mayan astrology. This additional aspect is there to help you make the best use of each day. Each day lord also has a direction. There are four directions. Each direction is associated with a color: red for the east, yellow for the south, blue for the west and white for the north. Each day lord has days that are extremely supportive for them. Each of the twenty day lords also have days that have the potential to bring conflict or opposition. When the day lord for the present day is the same direction or color as your personal day lord, it is an empowering day.

Ian proclaimed to me, after finding out my birthday, that my day lord was Wind. IK, which is the word for the day lord Wind in the Mayan languages, represents communication and movement. My number was two. My number represented balance and duality. I was someone who was good at communication and liked change and variety. My number gave me balance, so that I was not unstable, as those who move about like the wind can often be. Wind belonged to the direction of the north, which was white. When it is a white day, or a day that is ruled by a day lord of the north, such as

Dog or Jaguar, then I am at my greatest power. When it is a red day, or day of the east, that is ruled by day lords such as Serpent and Reed, it is a supportive day for me. Blue or west days may be filled with surprises for me. Yellow days or days ruled by the south are opposition days, where I find my greatest challenges.

    Ian said that his day lord, the Star, was from the south, so he was the color yellow. The Star described Ian as someone who is argumentative, idealistic and seeks balance. His number, 11, also indicated that he was impatient and liked to take strong action. Ian was in opposition to me, because his direction was south and mine north. Our relationship was predicted to be challenging. I found out later that many relationships are comprised of people who are opposite directions.

    The place where all this information is maintained is called the Tzolkin. In English Tzolkin means count of days. It is considered the sacred calendar of the Maya. The Tzolkin is the first calendar that the Maya created. It is a perpetual calendar, which means that it cycles indefinitely, back to the beginning, every 260 days or nine months. It helps the Maya to be in harmony with the energy or light that comes from the center of the Milky Way. To this day, the Maya use the Tzolkin to keep track of what days certain ceremonies need to be performed. The Tzolkin has the ability to help you understand yourself and how your energy interacts with each day. This is the knowledge that Ian desired to share with the world.

    With the charts and tables Ian had invented, it was now easy to access and use the information stored in the Tzolkin. One could discover one's Mayan astrology day lord and number, which is equal to your sun sign in Western astrology, with little effort. He told me that when he had met Luna Bliss, she was using a very complicated system to determine a person's day lord. He showed me her book and all the complex charts that needed to be used to find the day lord. I was overwhelmed just looking at all the calculations I would have to make to figure out my day lord. However, when using Ian's charts, it took less than a minute.

I found everything Ian was talking about to be very appealing. I was a great fan of Western astrology. Being a self-taught person, I had read many books on astrology and had learned how to cast an astrology chart and obtain helpful information from it. Western astrology or Gregorian astrology offers different information than Mayan astrology. I felt that both systems could be very useful. I see now that Western astrology focuses on the impact that the planets in our solar system have upon us. The Maya, however, even though they were aware of the planets in our solar system, chose to make the focal point of their religion and mythology the center of the Milky Way, which they called the Hu Nab Ku.

After he had spent about an hour educating me about Mayan astrology, I felt it was time to get on to the Therapeutic massage. That night we talked about our spiritual beliefs as I dug my elbows and knuckles into his back. It was a pleasant evening for me, but painful for him.

His body was very attractive. His skin was darkly tanned. He had long, lean muscles in his legs and arms. His broad shoulders narrowed to a small waist. From the rich, brown color of his skin, it was obvious that he loved to lie out in the sun.

After about 45 minutes of torturing him, I felt it was time to end the massage. He could take no more. I left the bedroom quickly, while he was still on his stomach. When he came out of his bedroom, into the living room, he was wearing a white linen robe that subtly revealed his body underneath. He escorted me into the kitchen where we had some water. He gave me a beautiful ring that fit me perfectly. It had designs all around the band and a bright stone of Orange Aventurine in the center. When I had gathered up my things, I headed for the door. He went to the door to open it for me. As he opened it, he said, "You and I should become lovers."

I was startled by this statement. I was surprised and delighted at the same time. I did not want to show him how happy I was. I was pleased that he wanted our connection to be sexual and romantic. He didn't touch me or even kiss me that night, but we made plans to get together in a few days.

WHEN I CAME BACK TO THE TENT ROOM, THE SAME atmosphere prevailed. We went out to dinner before going in to his tent. During dinner he went on to describe more about Mayan astrology. Then he shifted to his own life. He felt he needed to devote himself to making Mayan jewelry, working with the astrology and his study of all that the Maya had left on the earth.

When we got back to his place and his pirate tent, the first thing he did was show me some of the jewelry he was making. I had to admit that it was noteworthy even though it did not initially excite me. I like jewelry that is rough, and asymmetrical, and his work
was very detailed and precise. It took a few weeks for me to be able to unite with the knowledge that the jewelry embodied. After being with Ian for a while, and looking at his jewelry over and over again, I began to see its attractiveness. That was because, by then, I knew what the jewelry represented. It was that understanding that gave it magnificence to me.

It is that same understanding that makes a person who is not gorgeous on the outside, beautiful to their lover. That is the alchemy that manifested between Ian and me. It became clear that I was not his type. I was not tall, blond and did not look like stripper, but he grew to love me anyway.

Speaking of strippers, after he showed me some of his jewelry, he pulled out a photo album that he just happened to have handy. He wanted to show me pictures from the time he worked as a male exotic dancer. With great pride, he placed a most revealing photo album in my lap.

This viewing hurled me into a process that I can only describe as checks and balances. A red stop sign was now flashing at full capacity in my head. I was at a crossroads. I didn't know if I should I go ahead and have a sexual liaison with him or run screaming out of his house. Ian was stepping back and letting me go through my process. He was giving me some time to come to my own conclusion.

He walked into the kitchen to get us some wine. I certainly needed it. He could see that my initial reaction was not, "Oh, how fantastic!" I do have to admit that I was bewildered. This was not typical second date information.

When Ian came back with two glasses of Merlot, he smiled and put the photo album away. I made no comments about the photos and neither did he. He brought out another photo album, this one filled with pictures of his jewelry. "What a relief!" I yelled out in my mind, as he showed me page after page of his artistry.

He was having a great time showing me the pictures of his jewelry and some bronze work he had done. He filled me in on the story behind each piece. I was having so many thoughts and reactions in my head. It felt like there was a stadium of screaming football fans in there. I knew that I had to make a decision in a few moments. Was I going to have sex with this man? While I was lost in thought, he excused himself to go to the restroom. I felt he was waiting for a ruling from me. One part of the jury inside me wanted to sit there and be numb. Another part of me wanted to run out the door before he got back from the bathroom. Another part of me was saying, "So what! What are you getting so upset about? Don't make so much out of this."

When he came out of the bathroom, I stood up, went to him, and gave him a long, expressive kiss. The third voice had won out.

That was the inauguration of our love life. And what a love life it was! Those first few months were filled with wonderful nights. Ian was engaging, interesting and more. It was our lovemaking that cemented me to him. It created a bond between us that kept me glued to him for the next two years of an astounding journey. Our time together would be recorded in my book of life as being the most powerful, magnificent and painful relationship I have had in my life so far.

SPENDING TIME WITH IAN WAS A BIT OF A CHALLENGE. He lived in the very south of Phoenix, and I in the very north. When I visited him we would talk about Mayan astrology in between our rounds of lovemaking. It was during these times that the knowledge that he talked about incessantly started to gel within me. In one of our first evenings together, Ian shared with me the way the idea for the conversion charts had come to him. While the candles flickered in his little tent, he enacted his story. The puzzle was floating around in his mind for a long time. He had seen the many charts and calculations that were necessary to be able to determine a person's Mayan day lord. The books that he had found on the subject made it very complicated to find one's Mayan astrology sign. Ian had left this problem in the recesses of his mind.

He was up in the clouds, over Houston, Texas when the method appeared to him. He said that he closed his eyes and in 15 seconds, the charts where there. He simply looked at them. He feels that he was given the information. He felt that he had been divinely gifted with it.

In Ian's mind, the Mayan teachers of the past came down and said, "Here you are Ian. This is what you have been seeking. Here is the knowledge that you are going to share with the world." I found out later, that Ian was born under the day lord that gave him a direct link to the knowledge of the ancestors. By the time he came down from the clouds, he had drawn out all the charts.

I loved to listen to him tell this story. He would talk to me on the phone for at least two hours a night when we weren't able to see each other. It was during those conversations that my love for him deepened. Even though the lovemaking was beyond my greatest hopes, it was the way he talked to me each night that made me feel loved.

AFTER IAN RETURNED FROM HIS TRIP TO MEXICO WITH Luna Bliss, Ian told me we were going to Santa Fe, New Mexico to do an Ayawaska ceremony. For those of you who are not up on the latest shamanic ceremonies, Ayawaska is a mixture of herbs that act as a ceremonial hallucinogenic for indigenous cultures of Central and South America. Shamans from Columbia were coming to New Mexico. He wanted me to experience the happening with him. Ian had found out about this event from a woman that he had been in contact with for some time. She was a Mayan healer and ceremonialist called Hortencia. She had many connections with authentic Mayan shamans and shamans from other cultures in Central and South America. Three shamans were coming to Santa Fe to share their herbs, music and healing. Ian was going there to sell his jewelry and connect with the shamans. The journey ended up being one where we walked through more than one world.

We left for Santa Fe in the morning. It was early in April. The weather was nice in Cave Creek and Phoenix, but as we entered the Colorado Plateau, a few miles outside of Flagstaff, the weather started to turn chilly. We were on the low budget trip. Ian and I would have to camp out, unless we could find someone to put us up. We were supposed to rendezvous with Ian's connection at a house outside of Albuquerque.

We were to stay at the house of a woman, named Claudia, who was an apprentice to a Mayan daykeeper called Don Alejandro. Later we found out that Don Alejandro was the head of the Mayan Council of Elders. She had stayed at his village up in the highlands of Guatemala. Claudia had learned how to do Mayan ceremonies, and had received a lot of Mayan teachings from this mentor. She had been through many traumas because of her studies, yet she was very devoted to the teachings and Don Alejandro. Ian spoke of her with high regard.

While we were going along Highway 40 that took us into New Mexico, he started to tell me more about Claudia. She had gone through many physical and emotional challenges to be able to do her shamanic training with the revered elder. We were to go to her house and then go to a meeting of the shamans who were from Columbia. We were also going to meet a shaman who served under Don Alejandro and helped supervise his students. We were not going to take the Ayawaska that night. This was just a get together to meet with the men who were going to do the ceremony.

Ian and I talked the whole way into New Mexico. We were enjoying ourselves immensely, when Ian suddenly realized that we were lost. We were engulfed in the fervor of our discussion and somehow missed an important turnoff. We didn't know how far out of our way we had come, or how far we needed to go back. We left the sphere of our conversation and started to focus on the little road in front of us. We were out in the middle of a deserted New Mexico road. Ian poured over his directions, and I just sat there. I felt that I was in a slightly altered state, but that was all that I could be sure of. I did not try to participate in figuring out how to get out of the situation we were in.

Ian decided to go back the way we came. Sounded good. Logical. It should be simple. Yet an hour later, we were no closer to finding the right road than we had been the first time we figured out that something was amiss on our journey. We turned around again. As we were about to proceed, Ian turned to me and said, "I feel that something is happening to us. I feel that we are in some type of altered state."

I had to agree with him. We both felt that we were all right, but we knew that something out of the ordinary was happening. It was something that we did not understand or have any control over.

I suggested that we just sit still for a few moments until we felt that we were able to proceed. We started to laugh because we didn't know what else to do.

We accepted the situation and waited in the car. After about twenty minutes, we suddenly felt that whatever had been suppressing us had been lifted. Something had shifted. "I feel something is different now." I said, "Yes", Ian said, agreeing with me, "Whatever has been holding us captive has let go. I feel that we can get to where we are going now." With that, Ian started up his red La Baron convertible. After about ten minutes of driving, we found the turn off that we had driven by twice and somehow didn't see. In about half an hour, we arrived at our destination.

THE LITTLE TOWN WE FINALLY FOUND WAS LIKE MANY OF the run down little towns that populate New Mexico. We finally pulled up to one particularly shabby, little house with weeds in the front yard and a chain link fence that made the whole house and yard look desolate.

When we got out of the car, Claudia came out of the house, went over to Ian and gave me a big surprise. She put her arms around him and gave him an enthusiastic kiss on the mouth. This of course, flipped me out completely. Claudia was a very attractive woman. She was tall, slender, and had long straight, dark brown hair. She also had pale, white skin that made a dramatic contrast to her large brown eyes. After she had pried herself out of Ian's embrace, she turned and walked into the house, gesturing us to follow.

I was impressed with the difference that the interior of the house had in contrast to the exterior. The house seemed to be one long narrow room with a kitchen, bathroom and bedroom adjoining the long room. As we came in, a woman was going out. Claudia turned to us and said, with a little laugh. "It's good that you didn't get here until now. I was doing some important work with my friend."

"Is that why we were wandering about in the New Mexico desert for hours?" I thought to myself. I was feeling a mixture of rage, powerlessness and a bit of awe for this woman. I knew that what she was involved in was real. It was very real. I also realized that I needed to keep my jealousy under control. I didn't feel this was a safe place to express myself.

I took a closer look at the items in the house. I felt drawn by the strength of the large collection of ceremonial paraphernalia that surrounded me. All the objects in the room had power. I walked closer to some of them and extended my hand over them. My hand started tingling when it went over a few of them. That was a sign to me that these objects were imbued with ceremonial energy. There was a wide assortment of bones, rattles, drums, beads, pictures, candles, sage, incense, feathers, claws and shells displayed on tables and hung on the wall. I felt attracted to certain objects. I realized that the entire side of one wall was a long, narrow altar. I knew that it would not be a good idea to touch anything; that much I had learned from my years of doing spiritual work. I looked back at Claudia. She was keeping an eye on me. She could see that I was being respectful of the objects and not touching them.

Claudia was not only good looking, but she was also very knowledgeable in a field that I knew little about. Her connection to this indigenous knowledge was able to keep people wandering on the road for hours until she was ready to see them. This was real power! I felt that it was some type of group consciousness that protected her and her endeavors. Maybe it was the remote viewing of the elders she was studying under that were keeping her from being interrupted. I did not know for sure. Something greater than Claudia was watching over her, that much I did know.

I was fascinated with this new world that I had entered. While I was looking at the altar, Ian and Claudia were on the opposite end of the living room. They were having a quiet conversation. I was trying not to notice. In a few moments they split apart and went to separate areas of the room. I got the impression-that later proved to be correct that they had decided to take a rain check on romance. I could sense that she was going to be respectful of my relationship with Ian. For the rest of our visit there, and for the rest of the time that she knew Ian and me, she kept her distance.

Her teacher, Don Alejandro, and her studies were her only concern. Don Alejandro was considered by many to be a Mayan elder that was honest and sincere. He was a man who many in the Mayan world respected. He had taken on the responsibility of teaching the secrets and the traditions of the Maya to a select group of people. I assumed his desire in doing this was to find people who were going to be able to carry on the teachings that he wished to share. Many indigenous peoples have realized that their own flesh and blood may not be the ones to carry on their traditions. They were allowing those from other cultures to learn their secrets. This was the way that the elders of the Maya and other traditions were keeping their knowledge alive. Claudia was one of those people that the Maya trusted with their secrets. Don Alejandro had his apprentices stay in his little village high in the mountains of Guatemala. They had to live with his people and know their lives. They had to merge with the spirit of the Maya to honor the teachings.

IT WAS GETTING DARK WHEN WE WERE TOLD THAT IT was time to leave her house. We were going to meet the shamans that had come from Columbia. Claudia, Ian and I piled into her car and she took us to a Circle K that was about thirty minutes away from where we were. We got out of the car and there were several Hispanic men standing at one end of the parking lot. They recognized Claudia and started waving. She quickly walked up to them. Ian and I walked behind her. We stopped in front of three very short men who had dark brown skin and straight, short black hair. They looked tired but were very polite. They were the elder shaman and two young shamans. They spoke no English and were just smiling and nodding.

One can only know that an event is fateful or important to one's life in retrospect. The well dressed, impeccably groomed, forty-something Latino man who came up to me was about to enter my life and transform it. A hand was being offered to me. It was the hand of the Mayan shaman, Alex Martinez. He was smiling at me and seemed very excited to see me. I felt honored that of the two of us, Ian and myself, he approached me first.

"I see a lot of geometric forms moving around your head." He said after introducing himself. He continued to stare at the space above my head. "They are very beautiful, like you. They are all different colors. The forms are hovering around you. I am very happy to meet you. You will go far with your work. You do many types of spiritual and healing work, don't you?"

I tried to keep my mouth from dropping open. I just smiled and nodded, like everyone else. For Alex Martinez to know all that about me was fantastic and creepy all at the same time. These people were really impressing me. I felt very humbled. Even more humbled than I had felt at Claudia's house. I knew that for whatever reason I was brought here, I was connecting to knowledge that was very impressive. I guess the geometric forms that were swirling around my head were impressing Alex. He kept staring at the area above my head for a long moment. "Very nice" he said, and then moved on to Ian.

"So, you are the man who is very involved in the Mayan astrology, the Tzolkin? Ian shook his head in agreement. He knew that he was in the presence of a formidable person. This awareness humbled Ian. When Ian was in the proud mode, he would puff out his chest like a bird doing a mating dance. Now, he bowed his head while he was talking to this man who was at least half a foot shorter than him.

Alex and Ian had a quiet conversation for a few moments. There was some kind of bonding going on between them. They had not met each other before, but I felt that they were very close from the beginning. Then we were all told to get back in the car. Alex and the three Columbian shamans got into a car and sped away. We got into Claudia's car and went off in another direction. We ended up back at Claudia's house. Claudia retired to her bedroom and left us to sleep out in the long, narrow living room.

MY DREAMS THAT NIGHT WERE IMPRESSIVE. I HAD several. It felt like I was watching one movie after another. The strongest dream was about a jaguar. The dream started as I was walking on a suburban street filled with houses. Ian was with me. Suddenly, a hole opened up in the asphalt. It looked like a long tunnel had come up through the paved road. From out of the tunnel jumped a full grown jaguar. It came out onto the street. It started to lunge toward me. Its claws were out and its jaws open. I was terrified that the jaguar was going to kill me, so I picked up a nearby rock and hurled it at its face. The rock hit the huge cat in the middle of the forehead and stopped its lunge toward me. It fell down and was bleeding. Ian and I walked over to it. Ian said that it was dying. I knelt down and put my hands on the jaguar. I felt its essence go into me. I stood up and I noticed that the jaguar's markings were superimposed upon my body. I suddenly had a jaguar tail as well.

That dream merged into another one where I was in a kitchen and did not know what I wanted to cook. I was in a rather austere kitchen. Everything was white: white tile, white floors, and white furniture. I was looking around in all the shelves and cupboards trying to find something to cook. As I opened the cupboards, I could see that the shelves were brimming over with colorful food. There were a lot of fresh fruits and vegetables. I found a big salad bowl and began to make a salad. When I was done, I found a pair of wooden salad forks to toss the salad. I put some dressing on the salad. When I started to toss it, the salad turned into butterflies. Suddenly the whole kitchen was filled with butterflies that flew out the kitchen window.

The last dream that I remember from that night was a scary one. I was standing next to a big pit. It looked like it had no bottom. I was standing on the edge, looking down. Suddenly, the pit started to move. It turned into a dark, tornado-like funnel. I could see it whirling faster and faster. Suddenly I was being pulled into it. Then I woke up. I woke up puzzled and scared, but I was not surprised. I knew that I was in a powerful place, so I accepted that my dreams would also be remarkable.

I woke up first that morning. I just let Ian sleep while I thought about my dream-filled night. He woke up about ten minutes later. After I felt that he was awake enough, I started to whisper to him. I didn't want to wake up Claudia. When I told him about the jaguar dream, he started to chuckle. "It sounds like you had a run in with your Uayeb."

"What is that?" I asked, full of curiosity.

"A Uayeb is a spirit guide or a totem animal. Everyone has one, but we usually don't see them. They are your counterpart in the underworld. They usually just come out during the Uayeb days at the end of each Mayan year. The end of each Mayan year on the solar calendar is a time that is like a void. It is when the old year is destroyed and the New Year begins. It is considered bad luck to have a baby or to start new projects at this time. The Maya of old did not light their cooking fires during this time. The Mayan New Year started a few weeks ago. It is not time to see the Uayeb right now. I think they may be hanging around this house, though. Anything could happen here!"

I shook my head in agreement as we started to get up and get organized for the day.

THE THREE OF US WENT OUT TO HAVE BREAKFAST AT one of the local coffee shops. It was quaint and the food was good. That breakfast started my obsession with New Mexico red sauce. The savory chili sauce really made my eggs taste great! After breakfast we went to the place where Alex was staying. It was a small house with a large plot of land. Claudia told us that she and the other apprentices were going to practice a ceremony. We followed Claudia into the small house. She was going to show us how to do the ceremony. It must have been all right with Alex, because he saw Claudia talking to us and showing us how to make the ceremonial plate. I wanted to learn anything that they were willing to teach me.

The ceremonial fire offering started with a base of a ceramic, terra cotta plate. It was like the water dish that you put under a terra cotta planter. The plate was shallow and about a foot in diameter. Claudia had brought the plate and all of the ingredients with her to this gathering. She took all the objects out of a special bag. I felt the energy building in the room as all of the apprentices got closer to finishing their ceremonial plates for the Mayan Fire Ceremony.

Claudia covered the bottom of her plate with a layer of sage. After each layer, a sprinkling of rum was added before the next layer was placed on the plate. The candles were next. The candles were of a specific size and shape. They were small, about four inches in length. What was interesting about them is that there were four of each color: red, blue, yellow and white. The candles were placed in a certain order on the plate, which I assumed corresponded to the four directions. The concept of honoring the directions of north, south, east and west was an important part of most indigenous ceremonies. The wicks of the candles were all pointing to the center. Next, more rum was sprinkled on the pile, then a layer of sage and more rum. The last ingredients that came to rest on the plate were dark bits of Copal, or tree resin. Copal is similar to the incense that is used in the Hindu and Buddhist faiths. Finally the ceremonial plate was topped off with another dash of rum and a final layer of sage.

Now the plate was ready to go. Claudia took her plate to the area where the other apprentices were waiting with their plates. They were all standing around in a group, holding their plates and whispering until Alex came toward them. As he walked toward them there was a definite change in the group mood. They all shifted their attention to their mentor. Now the apprentices formed a line while their teacher watched them. They all seemed to know what was expected of them: silence and order. We stood with Claudia at the end of the line. Alex had a very stern look on his face. He looked at Ian and me and did not smile like he had the night before. He came up to me and asked me if I was menstruating. Having my "moon time" was the way that Native Americans usually put it. He said that it was very important that there were no women present who were bleeding. Fortunately, I was not having that problem. I was in the middle of my cycle, so menstruation was very unlikely.

Now Alex went to the front of the line. The apprentices were ready to go to the ceremonial area. The line of people, wearing bright Guatemalan attire, walked to an area that was about 500 feet from the house. Alex led the line to a place that had a large, circular pit dug out of the earth. The pit was about two feet deep and about a hundred feet in diameter. There were some stairs cut out of the earth that made it possible to go to the bottom of the pit easily. This pit had been constructed to specific dimensions, Claudia told us later. There was one plate sitting in the pit and it was covered with snow. We were all silent as we went into the pit. I dared not say anything. Soon all the apprentices were arranged in a circle within the pit. They placed their terra cotta dishes down on the ground in front of them and then sat down on the earth. Claudia sat down, and we seated ourselves at her right side.

Alex reiterated that if there were any women that were bleeding, they needed to leave now. Alex wasn't looking directly at me, but he did say that again. I felt a little self-conscious because I was the only woman who was new to the group. The group was made up mostly of women. There were only a few men.

We waited for the ceremony to begin. All of the apprentices and Alex started to chant. The language was not Spanish. I assumed that they were speaking a Mayan dialect. I did not know what was being said, and no one bothered to translate. I kept my head bowed, because I felt that prayers were being offered. Then, all at once, the apprentices set their plates on fire. There were a few moments of silence as the flames reached up toward the sky.

Alex was walking around inside the circle, looking at all the plates, his hands clasped behind his back. As the plates were burning, Alex came around to us. He pointed to the plate that was half burned and covered with snow. "The person who made this plate was very evil. Her plate did not burn. I had to ask her to leave the circle. The ingredients are still sitting there. They will need to be removed before our next ceremony."

We sat watching the fire for about half an hour. As the plates burned, all were silent. All the apprentices were either staring at their plates or had their eyes closed. Claudia did say something to us when her plate of magical ingredients was almost completely consumed by the fire. "If the terra cotta plate cracks when the fire is lit, that means that the offering was not accepted. Fortunately, none of my plates have cracked so far."

When all the plates had ceased to burn, we were all allowed to leave the ring. A circle of blackened, terra cotta plates were left in the ceremonial area. One at a time, we filed out of the pit. All of the apprentices left the area in silence. I did not want to say anything, even though I was full of questions. We rode back to Claudia's house in silence. I wanted to be respectful of her needs and did not ask questions. I received no further information about the ceremony from Claudia or anyone else.

That afternoon I gave Claudia a massage. Her lower back was hurting her. I really didn't feel that I had accomplished much when the massage was over. She, on the other hand, felt that something powerful had happened during the massage. She said that the pain in her back was completely gone. This is rather unusual in the massage world. It usually takes a few sessions to get good results. I have had the experience several times, however, that people were healed after one session. I have always felt that in these cases, there was something more going on than just the massage. I have felt that a greater force was helping me. When Claudia got up from the sofa she was lying on, she expressed that her back was healed. She had experienced some of my own brand of healing magic. She said that she was having pain from sitting in ceremony for many hours at a time. Now she felt that she was feeling good enough to participate in the Ayawaska ceremony.

THE FOLLOWING EVENING, WE WENT TO THE LOCATION where the Ayawaska ceremony was scheduled to take place. It was happening at a house that was in Santa Fe proper. We had been told to eat lightly that day. I thought that it would be good to drink juices, but Claudia wanted to go out to breakfast. For the rest of the day, I drank only water.

When the evening started to appear, around 5 o'clock in the afternoon, we started to get ready for the Ayawaska experience. We were to wear comfortable clothes. I had been to an Ayawaska ceremony before, so I knew a bit of what to expect. Soon after dark, Claudia, Ian and I left for the place where the Ayawaska journey was to take place. Ian and I followed Claudia to the location. When we stopped, we were in front of a small house in the countryside. A few trees surrounded the house. As I walked through the front yard, I noticed that there were deep pits dug at the base of the trees. I thought that was a bit curious, but later I found out what the pits were for: vomit.

We came into the house and met the hostess. She was a rather tall woman who was a photographer. She was soft spoken and pleasant. Slowly, the rest of the people came. In about half an hour, Hortencia arrived with the three shamans. They were wearing their street clothes like the rest of us. We were asked to stay outside while the shamans prepared the room. When we entered, about a half hour later, the room had been transformed. All the furniture had been put in the bedroom. The house was small and had only one bedroom. The shamans were dressed in their ceremonial attire. They were naked except for shorts. They all had on headdresses with many vivid colored feathers in them. Their bodies were painted with designs. They had created an altar on the ground. A piece of brightly colored cloth was the base of the altar. Upon the cloth were many objects. As we all filed in, we passed the altar that had a bowl of the herbal mixture we were about to ingest, as well as rattles, flutes, feathers, little statues and a wide variety of ceremonial objects.

Ian and I found a place on the floor that was big enough to lie down on, and laid out blankets. There must have been about twenty people in the room. It was big enough for everyone to lie down, but the quarters were close. We had to walk over each other when we needed to go outside.

The shamans came around to each of us with little cups of the sacred herbs. I treated it like a shot of Tequila and ingested it in one quick movement. I washed it down with some water I had handy. It doesn't taste as bad that way, and you don't have the continual gag reflex that often comes up when you are sipping something that is foreign to your throat and taste buds.

About a half hour after I had taken the liquid, I started joining the others in throwing up profusely. One was supposed to dash to the holes that had been dug out at the base of the trees when the urge came upon you. The hostess had said that it was good to offer the Ayawaska back to the earth. She had hosted several of these journeys before, and had given us all our own personal barf bags. Some people threw up all night. I was fortunate in that I got most of that part of the journey over at the beginning.

After a visit to the trees I went back to my spot next to Ian and my journey began. Alex had instructed me to lie down and close my eyes. I did as I was told and found myself in a wonderland of color and movement. With my eyes closed, I began to see colored patterns move across my field of vision. All of the colors were vibrant and seemed to be like bright neon signs. Bright, colorful, moving patterns glided across my mind. I did not know what was really happening, I just laid back and enjoyed the show. I could not focus on any of the patterns. They seemed to move quickly across my personal, mental movie screen. Just when I started to focus on the moving objects, they would start to change shape. At one point, I saw what looked like yellow rubber ducks moving across my mind. It reminded me of those outings to the carnival, where the ducks or birds were moving from one side to another and you tried to shoot them with a gun. The creatures changed every few moments, but they always kept moving in a line across my field of perception. In the background were brilliant light patterns that were blinking, shifting and twirling. It was a fantastic visual display, to say the least. This went on for what seemed like a few hours. Then I had to go outside again.

When I returned, the two younger shamans were making music with flutes. I also saw that the elder shaman was painting designs on participant's bodies with a brush and dark green paint. The paint seemed to be an herbal mixture. I asked Alex about this and he said that the shamans were painting protective symbols on anyone that desired it. The symbols were different for everyone that was at the gathering. They were placed on the arms, the chest and the hands. I watched many people do this and then I decided to take a turn. The shaman painted stars on my hands and arms. The dark green mixture stayed on my hands for several days through several washings. Ian received lightning bolts on his arms and hands. The shamans must have intuitively sensed Ian could bring through body lightning. Ian adored his lightning bolts. He raved about them for days.

After a while, the elder shaman started to do a healing ceremony on people who sought it. I decided that I wanted to try everything, so I got in line to get a healing. I sat with my eyes closed while rum was blown on my body. During healings, it is traditional for the shaman to take a large swallow of rum in their mouth and then spray it over the client. He also said prayers over me. I soon got into a very relaxed state and began to see the parade of images come back to me. In about ten minutes, the shaman tapped me on the shoulder and gestured to me that my healing was done.

I went back to my spot on the floor, next to Ian. I laid back and was able to see the neon parade continue. Every once in a while, I would open my eyes and look over at Ian. I was curious to see if he was having any experiences. I did not see any reactions from him the whole time.

When the daylight began to appear, I was over the hallucinogenic part of the journey. I was experiencing agitation, which is normal at the end of an Ayawaska journey, but other than that, I felt radiant.

In the early morning, Alex came over to me and asked me what I had experienced. I told him that I had seen very stunning colored patterns. I was about to continue, to elaborate on what I had seen, when he nodded in approval, smiled and said that I had a good experience. I had seen what I was supposed to see. He said that I was able to see what the plants were showing me. I had united with the sacred herbs and had been successful.

Ian on the other hand, had not had a good experience. I could see that he was disheartened. He did not get good marks from Alex. I think that it disappointed Alex that Ian had not had a victorious experience. Alex said that Ian needed to take another journey. There was another Ayawaska session scheduled in the next few days.

DURING THE MORNING, WHILE PEOPLE WERE GETTING ready to leave, Ian brought out his jewelry to sell. He was an incredible sculptor. He had a whole line of jewelry that he brought with him to Santa Fe to sell.

When we first started spending time with each other, he walked me through the whole process. First he would find a picture that he wanted to copy out of a book. His books on the Mayan culture were like holy bibles to him. He showed me the pictures from the books and then showed me the three dimensional objects that he had created from the pictures. I was dumbfounded at the accuracy and the detail that he was able to reproduce. He had been an artist for most of his life.

The symbolism of the Mayan jewelry made it very special. Ian enjoyed presenting each piece and discussing it in length with perspective buyers. He had pendants, bracelets and earrings. Initially, the buyers did not seem attracted to the jewelry, but when they were informed about the meanings behind the jewelry, they always wanted a piece of the jewelry on their bodies.

One pendant that Ian was particularly proud of was called the Crocodile Tree. At the bottom of the pendant is the face of the crocodile, complete with teeth. Then the body of the crocodile morphs into a tree, with the Quetzal bird sitting on top of it. The pendant represents the evolution of mankind. The symbolism illustrates man's development from his primal state, which the crocodile represents, to the more evolved state represented by the Quetzal bird. When I knew what the pendant meant, I was pleased to wear it.

I wore his jewelry proudly in Santa Fe and was able to explain some of the symbolism to people. I helped him with his jewelry sales. It was an enjoyable experience for me. I had a great deal of reverence for his ability to create beauty. I was talented with my mind, but art is something that is still beyond me in this lifetime. When I met Ian, who could do something that I was not able to do, I was extremely impressed. I felt honored to be part of the process that brought his jewelry to others.

WHEN THE CROWD WAS GONE, IAN AND I WERE LEFT AT the Ayawaska house. Claudia would not let us stay at her house that night. Ian and I stayed at the Ayawaska house for another night. This time we weren't lucky enough to stay in the nice warm house. The hostess had been through this type of situation many times before. She told us that we could camp out in the back yard, if we wanted to stay by the house. Unfortunately, it snowed that night. It was the coldest night I have ever spent outside. Ian and I erected his tent and slept there. I really would not call it sleeping, however. I was in a sleeping bag but could not move. I had gotten warm in the one position I was in, and I did not want to move and risk getting cold again. I stayed awake for most of the night. This experience really wore down my resistance.

The next morning, we went back to Claudia's house and met Alex there. Alex took us out to lunch in downtown Santa Fe. He wanted to show Ian the plaza where all the Native American people sold their jewelry. Alex was very impressed with Ian's jewelry. He knew that it had power. He knew that the jewelry was able to connect people with the frequency of the Maya. It became clear that Alex wanted Ian to continue to make and sell the jewelry. Alex wanted to be a part of a jewelry business with Ian. There were many places that the jewelry could be sold in New Mexico.

I loved the feel of Santa Fe. I could sense the tradition that was embedded in the town. While we were walking around the town, I started to feel something going on in my body. A quick stop at the nearest restroom revealed a few blood spots on my underwear. I was menstruating. Now I would not be able to go on the next Ayawaska journey! I spent the rest of the afternoon in a slight panic. I was having a difficult time coming to terms with what my body was doing. I did not want to miss the next ceremony. I did not feel like sitting out the ceremony while everyone else was seeing yellow rubber ducks.

After Alex brought us back to Claudia's house she was there waiting for us. Alex told her that he wanted us to spend the night with her. He did not want us sleeping in the snow again. She begrudgingly let us spend the night in her living room again. When we entered her house, it was like being in an altered state of mind again.

I did have another jaguar dream that night. I was in a bed, in what appeared to be an old fashioned hospital. It looked like it was a hospital from around the time of World War I. I was sitting up and smiling in a neatly made bed. Suddenly, a nurse dressed in the style of the period came in. She had what appeared to be a baby, wrapped in a baby blanket. She gave me the baby. I unwrapped the little bundle slowly. In the blanket was a baby jaguar. The overall feeling in the dream was that I had given birth to a baby jaguar. Ian laughed loudly when I told him about the second jaguar dream the next morning.

"The Uayeb is talking to you, all right. That is your power animal. It would not have come twice if it wasn't important. The Jaguar is the most powerful animal in the Mayan world. It has no natural enemies. It is worshiped by the Maya and many other cultures of Central and South America. This is a really good sign, Abby. The Jaguar is here to protect you and teach you. You are definitely here to help with the birth of my work." That validation from Ian made me feel very good. It validated my belief that there was a reason why I had come there.

I hoped that I was going to be all right for the ceremony. We went to the breakfast place again that morning. By mid-morning, there was still no blood, so I felt that I would be able to receive the Ayawaska that evening.

WE WENT TO THE AYAWASKA HOUSE WITH CLAUDIA THIS time. We had brought all that we needed for that night, including Ian's jewelry. As we spread our blankets on the floor, we noticed that there were some new people entering the house as well as some repeats. Shortly after it got dark, the ceremony began. The usual announcement was made that no woman was to be there if she was on her moon time. I lowered my head when I heard that. I was not bleeding when the ceremony began, but I was a little worried that the red demon might return to plague me.

I took the drink that was offered to me. Almost an hour had passed, and I was sitting there with nothing much happening for me. I had thrown up a bit, but other than that, I felt I was in my everyday state of consciousness. I went to the bathroom and the blood had returned. I went to Claudia and asked her to take me back to her house. She was firm and a bit angry when she said that she would not take me back there. It was almost an hour drive each way, and she would not leave. I sat next to Ian and continued to feel pretty much nothing.

I started to notice that no one else was experiencing anything either. The shamans were playing their flutes and rattles, but all the participants were looking at each other, shrugging their shoulders. No one was having any type of shamanic journey. The shamans started to look around. They also sensed that something was wrong. In a couple of hours, it was clear that something was very wrong. It was apparent that the sacred herbs were not giving their visions.

This awareness gave me a new admiration for the teachings and the knowledge that had been coming to me all that week. I had now seen proof that the ancient teachings were true. A woman's blood could halt the ceremonies for everyone. I could see that I was actually holding everyone back from having their journey. A few drops of blood had brought the whole journey process to an absolute halt for everyone. I kept looking at the shamans. I could see that they were truly puzzled. They did not know what was wrong. Only I knew what was wrong. I looked at the shamans several times. They did not know it was I who was creating the problem. The music of the flutes stopped. Everyone was checking with each other. Not one person was seeing the rubber ducks.

Even though the shamans and those taking the journey did not know what was wrong, the medicine of the plant knew what was wrong. The Ayawaska itself knew that the ancient law had been dishonored. The herbs knew that someone was violating the rule that had been set into motion eons ago. The plants would not give anyone visions. They would not share themselves until the one who was breaking the rule was no longer in the room.

I felt very gloomy and guilty. I was being selfish and keeping everyone from having their experience. I got up and pretended that I was going out to heave. What I did was start crying outside. I was crying because I was being denied another vision. My body was going through something strange. I cried because I could not be with Ian. Instead of going back into the main room, I went into the bedroom and began to cry even more. The hostess came in and asked me what the problem was. I said that I had started to menstruate. I told her that I would stay in the bedroom for the rest of the night. She did not reply. She just closed the door and went back to the ceremony.

Shortly after I entered the bedroom, I could feel that the energy in the living room had shifted. I heard the shamans playing their flutes. I heard people going out to vomit. I could hear people laughing. I heard Ian laughing. I felt that Ian was finally beginning to have a good journey. Finally he was experiencing the benefit that the herbs brought to our spirits.

That night I was given a message. While I was sitting in that little bedroom, sprawled out on the bed, crying giant puddles of tears, I heard a voice say that I was going to be separated from Ian. I would not be with him for long. I was being told that he had to go on his journey without me. I could not go with him the whole way. He had to do many things on his own, or with others. To a woman who has found love for the first time in a long time, this was devastating. I kept crying tears of grief and sorrow. I was crying tears for the loss that had not happened yet. I was crying for the lost love that I had just found.

This was a difficult message to accept. I did know that it was true, however. For I knew that the herbs were strong and that they were telling me a truth, a truth that I did not want to know. I did not know when this separation was to take place. I hoped that it would not happen for a while.

On that night I was told that Ian had a destiny. It involved much more than me. I knew that Ian's future was now in the hands of the ancestors. Ian was their messenger. There would be others who would help him with his divine mission. I was told, as the night went on, that I should just be grateful for the time we have together. I should not worry about what was to come. Throughout my life I had received enough demonstrations from sacred herbs to trust the messages that they were giving me that night. I could not grieve about what was to come. I should enjoy the moment. The herbs were keeping me awake and talking to me, but they were not giving me visions, only words.

I stayed in the bedroom until the dawn came. By that time the music, the healings and the visions in the other room were over. I felt that it was safe to come out of my lair. When I went out to greet Ian, he had a big smile on his face. He had been gifted with visions! He had told Alex of his visions, and Alex was proud. Alex was satisfied that Ian could continue to work with him. All was well. Alex was pleased and felt that Ian was coming along under his tutelage. Everyone was happy but me. In my next life, I am definitely going to be a man!

IAN AND I WENT TO THE CAR AND WERE TAKEN BACK TO Claudia's house. We quickly gathered our possessions that were in her house and said good-bye. Then we got into Ian's car and went to Hortencia house in a suburb of Albuquerque. We spent the night with Hortencia and the three little shamans.

Ian and I passed the night on Hortencia's living room floor. I have to say that I admired her a lot. She was a heavy set Hispanic woman in her mid-40s. She had a great presence about her. I felt that she was good at what she was doing. She poured a great deal of passion into her work. Hortencia was like a mother to the shamans. She made sure that the money that was collected went to them. She said that they needed to buy a boat. That was what the trip was all about for them. They came to this strange land to share the gifts that Spirit had given them in hopes of making their world better.

The next morning, we needed to say goodbye and return to Arizona. Before we left, Ian gave Hortencia a piece of jewelry that was an original. He gave it to her knowing that he could never make another because he had not made a mold for it. He gave it to her out of the respect he felt for her. The piece was called the Corn Maiden. It was a woman emerging from inside of an ear of corn.

There were to be more gatherings that summer. Don Alejandro, Alex and Claudia's teacher, was to be a speaker at gatherings in Santa Fe that summer. Hortencia said that she wanted us attend.

I was quiet on the way home. At the beginning of the seven-hour journey back to the Phoenix area, Ian was doing most of talking. He wanted to tell me all the details of his visions. He talked for probably an hour about his Ayawaska journey. He went into vivid descriptions about what he saw in the journey, how proud Alex was of him and then how well their connection was developing. He had given Alex a copy of his charts to look at. He was eager to get some good feedback from him. He was also hoping that this would mean the beginning of a great association with Alex.

During the drive, I dosed off a bit. I hadn't slept well for several nights. The nights at Claudia's were the only times that I slept well. Ian began to notice that I was not bubbling over with my usual effervescence. He started to have sympathy for me. He stopped talking to me. I fell quickly into that half-awake, half asleep state that one falls into when sleep is not entirely possible.

After what seemed like a couple of hours I woke up in the car with a start. I remembered a channeled picture I had painted many years earlier. I now knew who the man was in the picture: it was Ian!

Fifteen years before I met Ian, I had done an experiment with my channeling. For those of you who are not up on the latest New Age jargon, a person who is a channel allows a spiritual being to take over their body and impart inspirational messages. My channeling started when I lived in Mexico in the 1970's. At the time I did the paintings, I had been doing very little with my channeling. My life was not focused on spirituality as it is now.

In the mid 1980's, the woman who was teaching a past life regression class I was taking told me to do some automatic painting with the channeling. She said that I should give the entities a chance to express themselves through me as art. That would be nice, because I had zero natural ability for drawing and painting.

I decided to give channeled paintings a try. I purchased a bunch of acrylic paints and a pad of canvas paper that could be used for small paintings. Along with the other art supplies, I got some brushes. When I was ready to go, I squirted out a bunch of different colors on a paper plate that was next to the canvas. After a few deep breaths, I closed my eyes. I put the brush in my right hand. I wanted the channeled energy—if there was going to be any—to come through a different hand than the one I used to write.

As I started to relax, the energy started to flow through me, just as it does when I do a verbal channeling. I relaxed fully and whoever was painting started to take over. The entity dipped the brush in colors and then moved the brush over to the page. It was happening very quickly. My arm was making very rapid movements. For about an hour and a half, I kept my eyes closed and let the energy, the brush and the colors do their jobs. I kept my eyes closed the whole time. I felt that if I tried to peek, I would spoil the whole thing. I felt like a puppet, being moved around by a mystery painter.

Abby's channeled picture of Ian.

    Then the painting/channeling stopped suddenly. When I opened my eyes, there really was a picture in front of me. It was not just a blob of colors, but it was a very well done painting. The artist, whoever it was, had used an intriguing combination of greens and browns. It was a picture of a man's face. The man seemed to have long, dark hair, a beard and a moustache. The picture was able to convey the emotions that were within the man. What astounded me the most was the expression in the man's eyes. He looked like he was thinking about something that weighed heavily upon his heart. When I was finished with the picture, I did not receive a message about it. I had no idea who the man was.

I had put the pictures away for many years. I felt they were important, but I did not know why. I always kept them with me. There was a collection of eight paintings that had emerged through this process. Ian's picture was the first to emerge. I didn't know what any of them signified. It looked like the pictures were painted by different artists. One of the pictures was of a Phoenix bird rising out of its ashes. I was living in California at the time I painted them. I did not know that years later I would be living in the city of the Phoenix bird, Phoenix, AZ. In that quiet place that I was lulled into during the long car ride, after I was so fatigued that my resistance was lowered, I was able to dive into some part of myself that had something to tell me. "One of those pictures you allowed to come through you all those years ago was a picture of Ian." When I had the realization about the picture, I had to tell Ian. "Ian, I painted a picture of you about fifteen years ago!" That was all that I could say at the time. He just nodded and kept driving.

I was eager to find the painting and see if it was Ian when I got home. I stayed awake for the rest of the journey back to my home in Cave Creek. We got back in the late afternoon. Ian decided to go on to his place in Gilbert. We both needed some space. The journey had been very tiring for both of us. I was feeling very weary. I was, however, planning on conducting business as usual, which meant massages the next day.

THE DAY AFTER I GOT BACK FROM SANTA FE, I STILL felt drained. I felt heaviness in my chest. I went to the local doctor, a woman friend of mine, and asked her if she would examine me.

"You have some type of infection in your lungs. I need to give you some antibiotics." After a few moments, she came back with a shot. I went home and actually tried to work. When I collapsed a day later, she had me come into her office again.

"Abby, you must stop working for a week. You have a very serious infection. If I hadn't had this shot to give to you here in the office, I would have had to put you in a hospital. You are in bad shape. You will get over this, but you have to go home and rest."

The trip to Santa Fe had been too much for my immune system that was used to a mild, warm climate. It would take three of the shots to kill the infection completely. I went home and thought long and hard about Ian. I found that I was very angry at him. He had put me at risk, and I got ill. My bill at the doctors' office was over $1000. 00. I did not have health insurance at the time, so the doctor let me work off my bill by giving her and her family massages.

While I was resting that week, I was thinking a great deal about the whole situation. I hadn't gotten my usual nightly phones call from Ian that week either. I was too sick to call him and stay on the phone for a couple of hours. I was seriously reconsidering my involvement with him. Part of me said that it was not good to be with a man who could put me in a situation where such an illness was able to manifest within me.

IT WAS OVER A WEEK BEFORE HE GOT IN TOUCH WITH me. He said he wanted to come over to my place and talk. When he came over, he told me that he had received some distressing news from Alex. The shaman had told him that his count of the calendar was wrong. This meant that Ian's calculations for using the Tzolkin, the sacred calendar, determined that today was Tuesday, the 15th. This other group of shamans, namely Alex and Don Alejandro, said it was really Friday, the 11th. This is what was meant when Ian said that his count of the calendar was wrong. According to a reputable source, Ian's charts were configured to the wrong day.

I could see that Ian was going through his own trauma. That information would be a blow to me. It is upsetting to put all your hopes into something and then find out that it was incorrect. Ian really needed my support. He was facing a conflict that was devastating to him. He had started out trusting the count of the calendar that he had learned from Luna Bliss. He was selling her books. He had a lot of faith in her. She, in turn had gotten her count of the calendar from Jose Arguelles. There was really no other source of information readily available to tell people that there was another way to calculate what day it was on the Tzolkin. After all, we don't have a conflict over what day it is in the Gregorian calendar. Everyone knows what day it is all over the world with the Gregorian calendar. Why would the Mayan Tzolkin be any different?

  The people who were interested in this subject trusted Jose Arguelles. No one thought that there might be a quiet little group of Mayas living in the highlands of Guatemala that had different information. All the people that were interested in following the Tzolkin thought Jose Arguelles had the answers. He did, of course, start the Harmonic Convergence in 1987. That event put the Mayan calendar into the minds of millions of people on the planet. All of a sudden, this strange calendar was at the center of world attention. I had never heard of the Mayan calendar until 1987. I did remember seeing that the Harmonic Convergence had made the national news. Jose was there with his unique knowledge. Why would anyone doubt the accuracy of his findings?

  Alex had just burst the bubble that Ian had been living in for the last year. Ian felt that he had to listen to Alex. After all, Ian had seen a demonstration of Alex's power throughout the time we had been in Santa Fe. He had seen that many people felt Alex was an authority on Mayan culture.

  Ian needed to make a decision. Ian had to determine if he wanted to give himself over to Alex. Did he want to trust this new information about the Mayan astrology that had manifested for him? Ian had been offered the opportunity to spend time with Alex in his home in Northern California. Alex wanted Ian to come up there in a month or maybe less.

That night Ian had not yet decided if he was going to move to Northern California or stay here.

At the same time, I had been thinking a lot myself. I am a great believer in signs and omens. It is part of what I do. I had to admit that being involved with a man who put me in a situation to get very sick was perhaps a sign that I should not be with him. What kept coming back into my mind was the picture. I had found it when I had gotten home. It was Ian all right. Even Ian agreed, when he saw it, that it was him.

It was the picture that kept me allied with him. Even though I had been through a lot with the illness, which was a major stop sign, I also had a major green light come from out of my past, telling me there was something important about my connection to Ian. There was some reason that we were together. I was not clear on what my part was in this drama. I found out later that I actually had many parts to play; some of them were mother, lover, protector, chauffeur and muse. I decided to stay in contact with Ian and be open to what might develop.

That night was not like our usual encounters. There was no wild love making, and there was not much laughing. There was a good measure of melancholy. He did find it comforting to be with me, and I did feel better when he had his arms around me. We nurtured each other and found relief from our sadness.

A FEW DAYS LATER HE CALLED ME TO SAY THAT HE WAS moving to Northern California at the end of May. He had been busy making the arrangements necessary to move. We had resumed our nightly conversations, but I did not see him again for another week.

Alex was giving Ian a place to stay while they worked on realigning his charts to the correct day of the Tzolkin. Alex said that he had gotten his information and the count of the calendar from Don Alejandro and the Kiché Maya in the highlands of Guatemala. The reason for the discrepancy was that Jose Arguelles had used the most readily available information on the Tzolkin. This had come from the area of the Yucatan, in Mexico. The problem with the information from the Yucatan was that there had been many different influences in that part of the world over many centuries. What is now Merida had been a very busy sea port in ancient times, as it is today. Many tribes had conquered the inhabitants of the Yucatan and brought their own teachings to the area. That is how the count of the Tzolkin had changed over the years from the count that had been used by the Kiché Maya who lived in the Guatemala highlands.

The information from Alex and Don Alejandro is the knowledge that has been preserved by the Kiché Maya, in the mountains of Guatemala for centuries. The Maya who settled in this region were able to keep the count of the calendar from being corrupted by a lot of outside influences. They are considered, by many Mayan calendar scholars, to be the pure descendants of the original Maya.

Alex told Ian that he needed to redo his charts to reflect the correct count of the Tzolkin. Ian now knew that he not only needed to change the calculations that he had done, but that all this time he had been giving people incorrect information about their day lord. That is like being told that you are a Virgo. Then someone comes along that has different information. This source tells you that you are really an Aries.

Ian had to start from square one again. Well, not exactly from square one, but he needed to do some major adjustments. He needed to throw out all of the charts that he had printed up.

It was a very humbling experience for Ian. He soon began to see that it was all a blessing. He was being given a chance to make things right, to find the truth for his invention. He had been guided to a very pure source of knowledge. Now he was being given the opportunity to transform his creation.

In the month that followed, Ian enthusiastically set about getting his life in order. He did like to travel and was excited about going to a new location. He was going to live with an authentic Mayan shaman! He was ready to break down his tent and move north.

WHILE IAN WAS GETTING READY TO GO NORTH AND live with Alex, I was getting a pressure in my head. It was not a headache, it was the pressure that I get when I have to deliver a message and for some reason, I don't follow through. The message was that I had to introduce Ian to the man who had just made a web site for me. I kept having the nagging feeling that it was important that Ian meet my web master, Milt. This gentle and giving man had gifted me with a web site. It was 1998 and I didn't really know the value of a web site, but I was happy to have the gift. It made it easy for me to promote my channeling.

I knew that Ian was busy packing for his move, but I felt that I needed to express the idea of the trip to Payson to him. One night Ian had come over to my apartment for the evening. As we were settling down to sleep, I finally broached the subject of taking the 4 hour round trip up to Payson. As usual, Ian was polite and said he would think about going with me to meet the man who had designed my web site. Then he rolled over and went to sleep.

After another week had passed, and no plans or comments from Ian emerged about the Payson trip, I started to feel the message screaming in my head again. I am not a pushy person, but I knew that one message was not enough in this case. Ian was not listening to me. A few days later he came to my place and cooked a delightfully spicy dinner. As we lay in bed after a superb evening of love making, I reached over and put my arm across his chest and said gently,

"We need to go to Payson so you can meet my web master, Milt. You have to meet him. I feel that you need to have a web site." Ian smiled politely, nodded his head, and again turned over and went to sleep.

When I awoke the next morning, I kept hearing the screaming in my head: GO TO PAYSON!!!! OK,OK,OK!!! I kept muttering to myself, as I was getting dressed. As Ian was making coffee and contemplating making some breakfast, I realized that I would just have to get ugly. I would have to do the thing that I hate doing: I would have to yell, scream and do a lot of stamping around to get Ian to Payson.

As Ian was puttering in the kitchen, I walked up to him and started yelling " WE HAVE TO GO TO PAYSON! IT IS VERY IMPORTANT! YOU NEED TO MEET MILT AND GET A WEB SITE. WE HAVE TO GO TODAY!!!"

Ian stood there in the kitchen, a fork in his hand, in the midst of scrambling some eggs. He was shocked. I had never yelled at him before. I never would again. With bugged out eyes, and a look of shock on his face, he agreed to go with me that day.

I had called Milt. He was easy going and said it was fine to come up on the spur of the moment. It was during the week. Milt's wife worked all week and he always reserved the weekend for her and would not entertain company. This was really the perfect day to visit.

The pounding in my head about the message finally stopped as we wound our way up the narrow mountain road that started in Fountain Hills, a suburb of Phoenix. Even though I could feel Ian's attitude about doing something he didn't want to do, I could start to see the enjoyment in his face as he looked at the Pine trees and the change in landscape. He had spent a lot of time in Oregon and Idaho, and the Pine trees seemed to enchant him. I think he felt he would at least enjoy the scenery, if nothing else.

When we arrived at Milt's house, it was close to sunset. Milt and his wife, Kate, lived in a 2 acre compound in Payson. They had lived in Phoenix but were now aficionados of the forest.

When Ian walked into their house, his distinctive persona sent Milt's shy wife retreating to the far corner of their kitchen/living room. She stayed there for the rest of the evening, stared at Ian and did not say a word. Milt was really the more social of the two, and he was very polite to us both.

That evening, Ian and Milt didn't really say anything of consequence to each other. They seemed to just dance around each other, sniffing each other out like two curious dogs. Even so, I felt that my mission was complete. I had connected the two and then the two of them had to do the rest.

That night, Ian and I were back at my house, musing over the events of the day. We started to talk about names for the web site. He said that he wanted something about magic to be in the name of the web site.

"I want to call it Mayan Magic, but I don't want to use the word magic. How about majix?"

"I like that." I said "After all, IX, Jaguar, is the day sign of the shaman and healer. Jaguar represents magic, so I think having the day sign, IX, in the name is good. "I like that too. The web site will be called Mayan Majix!!" We cuddled for a long time and Ian thanked me for making him go to Payson.

Now www.mayanmajix.com recieves more than a thousand hits a day. It is a hub for information on earth changes, channeling, Mayan astrology and many other types of information for our changing times. It has become Milt's full time job. He has turned mayanmajix.com into a profound spiritual focal point and a place to find out about all things Mayan.

AT THE END OF MAY, IAN GATHERED ALL OF HIS BELONGINGS, including all of his jewelry making supplies, hooked up a trailer to the back of his car, and headed up to Clear Lake, California. There he would live with Alex and study the true count of the Mayan Tzolkin. It was a very sad time for me. I was just getting back into the swing of things. I was ready to invigorate our relationship, and now he was going away. I was deeply in love with him by this time.

Even though he was going, we were still keeping in touch. We were both very emotionally dependent on each other. We both needed the intimacy and the caring. He set off in his red Ianmobile, a Chrysler La Baron convertible, pulling behind him a trailer full of his jewelry molds and other jewelry making equipment.

In a way, I was glad to see him go. My financial situation had begun to go down hill when I started dating him. I see now that I had shifted my focus from making money to loving him. After he left, the money making got back on track. He was still e-mailing me on a daily basis. We weren't able to talk very much. Cell phones had not come on the scene in a major way yet.

Shortly after Ian had arrived, he emailed me that everything was going well with Alex in the sense that he was getting a lot of work done. He never went into great detail about what he was doing with Alex, but I knew that it was humbling for him. He had dedicated himself to Alex and was following his instructions. In less than a month, Ian and Alex had reworked the conversion charts, and they were now synchronized to the Kiché Maya count of the Tzolkin.

What he did share was his dislike for Alex's wife. He was constantly complaining about his living situation. After a short time, he was able to move to another house and set up his jewelry making there. He was still working with Alex even though he was not living with him.

During the time that we were apart, I was doing readings with my tarot cards about Ian. I had studied tarot cards for many years. I was given my first deck of tarot cards as a present when I first started living in Mexico in the 1970's. I had been taught to use them by a woman who was English. She had learned to work with the tarot cards at an occult school in England.

My first readings about Ian were fairly positive. However anger in the relationship between Alex and Ian soon began to show up in the cards. Even after Ian had moved into Jerry's house, who is a kind, soft spoken man, the tension between Ian and Alex continued. I remember laying out my cards one night and seeing that there had been an upheaval between Alex and Ian.

"Alex is not getting along with Ian?" I said out loud. This puzzled me. I couldn't believe it, but I knew that I was receiving correct information. He had seemed so nice. He presented the façade of a quiet, proper gentleman. Alex had appeared to be so sincere about helping Ian. What was the problem? Like most intuitive guidance, information comes in bits and pieces. I knew there was something terribly wrong, but the particulars were not coming to me.

I planned to visit Ian at the end of June. We both had a strong desire to be with each other. He was eager for me to come and see where he was living. It turned out to be an intriguing excursion.

WHEN I ARRIVED AT THE SAN FRANCISCO AIRPORT, IAN was there to pick me up. We had a fabulous lover's reunion. It was very romantic the way Ian braved the rigors of the city traffic to get me. After a traumatic getaway from the city that included many wrong turns, we made our way to Clear Lake and arrived at the little trailer that Ian now called home.

The place where he was living was enchanting. It was a little Silver Stream that was situated next to a creek. It was high summer. All the trees that surrounded his trailer were bestowing their green light upon us as the sun filtered through them. Ian had fixed up the trailer with his Mayan cloths and decorations. The tent effect was not possible, but the whole setting was captivating. I settled in comfortably right away. The next day, after a divine morning of lovemaking under the trees, Ian decided to tell me what was really going on between him and Alex.

Ian was furious. From Ian's perspective, he was being used by Alex. Ian felt that Alex was stealing his invention, the conversion charts. The tension between Alex and Ian had gotten very bad. He did not stay at Alex's home more than a few weeks before a move had been mandatory. The tension between Alex's wife and Ian had been equally bad. That morning, Ian went into a long monologue describing his last confrontation with Alex. He enacted every moment and repeated every word he had said. I remember thinking that it was sad that the situation had turned sour so quickly. I also found it heartbreaking that Ian had lost such a powerful person in the Mayan world as an ally.

Jerry, Ian's new host, was very, as they say in California, laid back. He was not offended by Ian's manner or attitudes. He had an old shed that he was letting Ian use for jewelry making. Jerry was a metal sculptor. He made huge metal artwork. He understood Ian's love of working with metal and the process that was needed to turn red wax into handsome silver jewelry. He gave Ian Carte Blanche to use his place as he needed. It seemed like Ian had finally found a place where he could be himself and also do his work.

Now, Ian was awaiting the arrival of Don Alejandro. He was coming to Santa Fe very soon. Don Alejandro was Alex's boss, so to speak. He was the man that Alex respected and ultimately answered to. Ian felt that he needed Don Alejandro's endorsement to give his work credibility. He was determined to get the revered leader's support to authenticate his work. Ian believed that with Don Alejandro's blessing, the Mayan Calendar and Conversion Codex, as he was now calling it, would be valued by the Maya and the rest of the world. Ian was now on a crusade. He wanted everyone who used the Arguelles count of the Tzolkin to receive the true count of the calendar: the Kiché Maya count. He had the truth, and he wanted everyone to have it.

After Ian had completed his story, he changed gears. He told me that he had a present for me. He went into the trailer and brought out a little piece of cloth. He gave it to me to unwrap. Inside the cloth was a shiny piece of silver. On closer inspection, I found it to be my new Mayan day lord. It was one Obsidian Blade. The Obsidian Blade was the mirror of truth. It reflected back the hidden side of a person or situation, so that one could see oneself or others clearly. The blade cut away illusion. It cut away falsehood so that the truth could be known. It was also the knife of the healer. To be free of illusion was to be healed. The number one represented the beginning of a matter. I found out later that being born on a one day was very powerful because it is the start of a Mayan week. One people usually start or are at the beginning of a situation and help it to be birthed. I was there at the beginning when Ian was given the True Count of the Tzolkin.

I had given him back the 2 Wind day lord piece of jewelry that he had originally given me, before I came on the trip. The new day lord he gave me was a gift that represented all the change that we had been through. I could tell that he was feeling very pleased and proud when he handed it to me. Ian's present was very meaningful, and I have it still.

Ian turned out to be 12 Ancestors. Ian's day lord, Ancestors, represents creativity: dance, art, music and song. Ian excelled in all of those areas. He could give a terrific Karaoke performance. The day lord of Ancestors also represented the warrior, hunter and king. Those that have Ancestors for their day lord can commune with the ancestors of the Maya. Now that Ian knew his true day lord, it energized his belief that he had connected with the ancestors when he received the conversion charts. Ian believed that they were helping him through this whole process. He was sure that it was the ancestors who sent him to Alex. His number, 12, was the number that gives understanding. A 12 person can apply this understanding to all their projects. It was Ian who was going to help the general public understand the Mayan Tzolkin.

Ian selling his jewelry at a Harbin Hot Springs Festival.

Ian had created his artistic rendition of the day lords before I met him. I had seen many representations of the Mayan day lords, but Ian's really resonated with me more than any I have ever seen. I loved his use of the flowing, curved lines for the glyphs.

One of Jerry's friends, Emily, came to visit for a few days. She has a sardonic sense of humor that I really liked. Emily and I became great buddies. We are still great buddies. She has been one of the friends that appeared in my life and still stuck around. I talked to her about the Flower of Life workshop that I was teaching at the time. She seemed very interested in the teachings and wanted to learn more about it.

After a week of lovemaking by the creek and feeling the intoxication of the fairy energy there, it was time for me to go back to my place in Arizona. I didn't want to leave. I didn't want to be apart from Ian. I didn't want to leave the fairy energy, but I had to.

I HAD ONLY BEEN BACK TO THE DESERT AND MY CATS a few days when I got an email from some people who wanted to have a Flower of Life class in Clear Lake, California. They were about twenty minutes from Ian! The Universe, which is my term for the powers that be, God/Goddess, etc., had provided a way for me to go back to Ian. The money from the workshop would be enough to get me up there and back. I felt absolutely vibrant when I told Ian about this. He was excited too, but for a different reason. Ian had talked to Jerry and Emily and they both wanted to learn the Merkaba meditation as well.

I was scheduled to come back to Clear Lake only a month later. Was that good or what! Something was moving me around like a chess piece, but I liked where it was pushing me. A few days before I was scheduled to return to Clear Lake, Ian called me. He wanted to come back to Cave Creek and live with me. I should have been excited, but I had a weird feeling about it. Part of me knew that he needed to leave Jerry's place. Ian was a lot to handle. I knew he probably did not have any other place to go. That didn't bother me either, but something was. When I got up there, I found out what was bothering me. Ian wanted to live with me, but he wanted to be celibate.

When he first told me, I felt like screaming ARE YOU KIDDING ME? We have been cavorting like animals in heat, and now you want to be celibate? All that I could think of was that something strange was going on within him. What I found out, after a great deal of pestering him for the truth, was that he was afraid of getting too involved. Weren't we involved?

I tried not to harp on it too much. I knew that we weren't going to be together that long. I had been told that in Santa Fe. He didn't know that. I was feeling disbelief. I had already agreed to let him live with me, so I didn't feel like I wanted to back out of the agreement. He had an unexplainable fear of being trapped with me. It was fine when we had our own places to live and were together or talking to each other constantly. Something about residing together permanently had put him into a state of high alert. He suddenly had all these rules that had to be followed for us to live together. He grilled me on them daily.

The night that he told me this, I lay in the bed next to him and tried to sense what was going on with him. I wanted to know what this fear was all about. The image that came to me was one of all his ex-relationships. I felt his ex-wife and all the exes after her were all in the bed with us. He was taking his fears about relationship and putting them into our situation. Now I understood. I could not force him to continue on in the way we had been. I needed to surrender to his fears as I had surrendered to his passion. I had to honor his feelings and make the best of the situation. I also had to pray that he would let go of his fears and let us live together in the way that was natural for us.

The next day was the start of the workshop. There were going to be four people taking it: Jerry, Emily and the other couple that I could only describe as eccentric.

When it was time to return to Arizona, Ian loaded up his trailer and we were ready to make the journey home in the

Ianmobile. The only problem, or shall I say mishap in planning, occurred when Ian made the decision that we were going home via Las Vegas and the Nevada desert. That may not sound like such a problem, but when you are traveling through the desert in July with no air conditioning in your vehicle, it becomes a problem.

After a night in a Las Vegas motel room that had a great air conditioner, I had to get back into the hot box and continue to have the hot dry heat blast my face for another eight hours. At some point, it was so pathetic, that it became comical. I started laughing uncontrollably and Ian joined in.

The highlight of the trip back was when he told me that we were going to the next Mayan gathering in Santa Fe. He wanted to go to reconnect with Hortencia and the other Mayan enthusiasts that he had met.

IAN AND I WERE ON THE ROAD AGAIN AFTER ONLY A couple of weeks back in Arizona. We went in his car again, but at least this time, the area that we were driving through was not as hot as Nevada. We arrived in Santa Fe in good spirits. We drove into the University of New Mexico campus and soon found the building where the conference was taking place.

All went well until Ian walked into the vendor's part of the conference. Alex was there and had his own booth. He had made copies of Ian's charts and was selling them. Alex was selling Ian's invention without getting Ian's permission or giving him royalties. Ian walked up to the pile of Alex's nicely laminated charts. He looked at them for a few moments, and then walked away. I was at another booth in the exhibit area. He found me and told me we had to leave immediately. I felt a bit scared as I quickly followed him out of the building. Once outside, Ian started to explode. "He stole my charts and he is selling them!" Ian said. We walked quickly to the car and got in. I got the impression that in Alex's mind, he felt he had the right to sell them. He had given Ian the correct information. In Ian's mind Alex was stealing his invention.

Hortencia saw Ian at the conference and saw that he was upset. Her first loyalty was to Alex, no matter if he was wrong or right. Ian realized that he was alone in his anger. None of the people that he had felt were his friends would take his side.

Ian drove us home and spewed like a volcano all the way. Mr. Fun had turned into Mr. Grump. I can't be too hard on him because he did have a lot to be upset about. Ian was a bit naive to think that Alex would not use the information at his disposal.

The morning after we returned, Ian went to my computer and sent Alex an e-mail full of rage. He talked about the e-mail for many days afterward, so I have the words memorized. It was a short e-mail, but it was full of venom. It said "NOW YOU HAVE DONE IT. NOW YOU AND YOUR WITCH WIFE WILL BURN!" After sending his e-mail, Ian got a lot of the fury out of his system. Ian knew there was nothing that he could do about Alex and the theft of his work. After a few days, he calmed down and was able to go on with his project of creating a format to sell his charts without looking back.

We started on creating the Mayan Calendar and Conversion Codex with the new configurations. I really enjoyed being part of this project. Ian and I would sit for hours looking through the pictures in all of his favorite books, to pick the ones that we felt were the best for the pictures on the codex. I was always impressed with the colors, the style and the meaning of the Mayan art. I loved the round curves and earth tones of the art. By then, by living and working on this project together, even if our bodies were not coming together in passion, our hearts were merging in an exquisite way.

When it came to designing the layout for the conversion codex, Ian valued and used my suggestions. We picked out a mural that we wanted to use for the background. When we faded it out, we found that it was the perfect background upon which to place the charts and instructions.

I also gave Ian my input on the names for the directions. I had more familiarity with Native American teachings, so he used my knowledge for the directions. We made the east beginnings. The west is traditionally the place of death, so we called the west endings. It is the entrance to the underworld. In most Native American cultures, north represents knowledge, so we labeled the north mind. The south is always the place of innocence in Native American traditions, so we decided to name the south body.

Then Ian and I worked together to create the poem that he placed at the back of it. He would write out what he thought he wanted to say and then I would give him feedback.

The definitions for the numbers or traits as well as the names and definitions of the day lords all changed after he got back from being with Alex. He used the names of the day lords that Alex had given him. Ian found out from Alex that the names of the day lords were not correct on his first charts. Ian changed them to the ones that the Kiché Maya used. We wanted the most authentic names to be used in the first official codex.

In those first few months that we lived together, Ian and I made many adjustments to the Mayan Calendar and Conversion Codex. I had a lot of free time. The massage business was slow in the summer in Cave Creek. As I look back on that time, I could see that he was coming to love me more. We were getting to know each other in a different way.

THERE WAS ANOTHER MAYAN GATHERING COMING UP in Santa Fe. Before the problem with Alex had manifested at the last gathering, Ian had been scheduled to have an audience with Don Alejandro. However, Ian was not able to keep his temper in check and had to skip his scheduled appointment. This time, Ian was going to Santa Fe as a calm, composed man. Don Alejandro was coming to Santa Fe again. Ian didn't want to miss this opportunity to show Don Alejandro the conversion codex and get his endorsement. Ian felt that it was paramount that he received the elder's validation to authenticate his invention.

When we got to the conference this time, there was a potent wall of negativity that hit us as we entered the large meeting room. I noticed that a great many people were staring at us. Hortencia came running up to Ian.

"Alex does not want you to enter here," she said, as she worked at catching her breath. "You sent him an e-mail that threatened and insulted him and his family. Now he doesn't want you to be here."

Ian was in a panic. "What can I do about this, Hortencia?" he asked. Tears were beginning to well up in his eyes. "Is there a way to fix this?"

"I will ask Alex if he will accept an apology from you. Go outside and wait on the steps." She left and started walking back to the main room. As we left, I caught a glimpse of Alex. He was staring at us with a cold, fixed expression.
We did as we were instructed and went to sit on the steps of the building. In about ten minutes, she returned.

"Alex said that you must make a public apology. You must do it in front of everyone. We will come outside to talk to you." Hortencia turned and walked back inside.

I knew that this was not my battle. Ian had to go through it himself. I just went off to a corner of the steps and let the show play out. Alex came out of the building with an entourage of about twenty people behind him. Ian was standing on the bottom step. Alex came down to the step above Ian. It was hard for me to see the emotion that was going through Ian. He was very hurt by this situation. He kept his head bowed and stepped up to Alex.

He lifted his head and there were tears streaming down his face. I knew that the emotions behind the tears were real. Ian did not want a moment of anger to ruin all that he had struggled to create. He told Alex that he was sorry that he had threatened him. He would not have the truth about the Tzolkin if it had not been for Alex. Their problems had always been personal. The connection that they shared about the knowledge was pure. I hoped that this experience would help Ian appreciate Alex for all that he had done for his work. Alex had been an invaluable part of the project. The truth about Mayan astrology was all that was important, not their personal conflicts.

After the apology was over, he and Alex shook hands. Then Alex and the other people went back into the building. Ian and I went into the building after about 15 minutes. It took Ian that long to regain his composure.

Ian went over to Hortencia and asked her when he could have an audience with Don Alejandro. Hortencia went to Alex. We did not see what Alex's reaction was. Hortencia walked slowly over to us. She said that Alex would not allow an interview with Don Alejandro.

"You cannot see Don Alejandro while he is here. Alex will not permit it." Hortencia said sadly and walked away.

Suddenly an acquaintance approached Ian and said softly, "Don Alejandro will be arriving at 2:15 p. m. today at the airport. If you get there and see him before he gets into the car with Alex, you can talk to him for a few minutes on his way out of the airport."

Ian got extremely animated when he heard that there was a possibility of talking to Don Alejandro, even if it was just for a few minutes. Ian ran back to the car and I hurriedly followed. We went directly to the airport in Albuquerque. We got there in plenty of time. We were able to find out where the plane was landing easily. We went to the terminal and waited. I was not extremely enthusiastic about this plan. Why? I was the one who had to talk to Don Alejandro. I was the one who spoke Spanish. I had been impressed into the role of communicator. My Spanish was not that great, but I was able to make myself understood. Those two years of mandatory Spanish in college happened a long time ago. I tried not to focus on my irritation. I needed to focus on getting my part of this mission accomplished. It was a good thing for Ian that I was in love; otherwise, I probably would have tried to get out of the liaison role.

We were right there at the gate where the passengers from Guatemala City started coming through. I started to feel like I was in a movie. Ian had come up with a plan of action. We were not going to face him when he got out of the gate. We didn't know who was with him. All we knew was that Alex was waiting outside the airport, at the curb to pick him up.

We stayed by the side of the exit door, to see who was with him. Ian knew right away which person was Don Alejandro. He had his picture memorized. When a short Hispanic man with a hat came through the doors, Ian got very active.

"That's him. That's Don Alejandro." He was pointing with his nose, not his finger. In a few moments, I was able to discern whom Ian was talking about.

Don Alejandro was escorted by a very tall, heavyset man who I felt was like a bodyguard. We let them pass us and then we sprang into action. We were following about five feet behind the prominent Mayan elder and his helper. We started walking faster and faster. We were able to catch up to them. We walked up from behind and Ian was able to get close enough to tap Don Alejandro on the shoulder.

Don Alejandro turned around and looked at us in surprise. He did not stop, but slowed down enough for me to walk next to him and talk. I had to start talking fast. Ian was right next to me as I walked next to Don Alejandro and recited my rehearsed speech. I said that Ian had a new system for finding the day lords and the numbers of the Tzolkin. I told him that Ian desired a meeting to show him the system. I said that it would help many more people be able to use the Tzolkin.

I put a card in his hand with our phone number and e-mail address. Now we were getting close to the exit door. I said Adios and Ian and I fell back. Don Alejandro put the card in his pocket as he walked out of the airport. I was able to accomplish what we needed to do. We watched Don Alejandro go through the doors to the outside, the curb and Alex.

We spent the night in a motel in Albuquerque. We decided to celebrate our victory of connecting with Don

Alejandro instead of dwelling on the humiliation that Ian had received from Alex. After a night of champagne, fry bread and playing in the motel's pool, we returned to Arizona.

BY THE TIME WE RETURNED TO CAVE CREEK, IAN WAS rejuvenated. He had talked out of his anger on the drive. He held on to his feelings of optimism. He maintained his focus of the possibility of having a meeting with Don Alejandro. He decided to be hopeful instead of doubtful.

After about two months, Ian decided to relinquish his vow of celibacy. We were in a friend's hot tub, up in the mountains of Payson, when Ian decided to let that go. Ian and I made love in the hot tub and in our little guest room. I guess he was making up for lost time. Anyway, we were back on track in the lust arena. FINALLY!

LIFE WAS LOOKING A LOT BETTER NOW. EVEN THOUGH I had foreseen the future for many people by that time, I put the cards away. I knew what was going to happen, but I wanted to keep my attention in the present. I was having a good time again. Ian and I were going to Mexico in a few weeks! Ian was now on a crusade to get the blessing of Don Alejandro for his conversion charts. Ian had received an e-mail from Don Alejandro. He was going to grant an interview with Ian at his home in Guatemala City in September.

I miraculously had enough money for the trip. Ian wanted me to go. He felt he would need an interpreter. I wanted to go back to Mexico for several reasons. I had not been back to Latin America for 25 years. I wanted to see the land and the people again. I had gone to college in Mexico and received my B. A. degree from the Universidad de Las Americas. I had a lot of great memories of Mexico. I also wanted to be part of Ian's work. I felt I was an important component in all that he was doing.

We were going to fly into Merida, in the Yucatan. The Yucatan was a term that was used for the large peninsula of the southern tip of Mexico. There Ian was going to meet up with Drunvalo Melchizedek who was the originator of the

Merkaba meditation. It was Drunvalo's workshop that had brought Ian and me together. Then we were going to some of the Mayan ruins in the area. Next we would travel to nearby Cancun for a few days. Ian and I both wanted to go to the ruins of Tulum. This was a beautiful Mayan ruin right on the ocean that had been occupied by the Maya when Cortez sailed by it. After seeing the sights in the Cancun area, we were going to take a plane to Guatemala City to meet with Don Alejandro. Then it would be back to Mexico to stay with a friend of Ian's that he had met at the Tucson gem show a few years ago. His name was Pablo. He lived outside of Cuernavaca, in a town that had been very important to me when I was in college. It was a little town called Tepoztlan. I found it remarkable that we were going to a town that I had gone to many times when I was in college in Mexico in the 1970's.

    In the same way that I had made a painting of him before I met him, Ian had also made a sculpture of me. After we had come back from Santa Fe the second time, he took me to meet one of his friends. She was a tiny little woman named Millie. Ian had sold her a piece of his artwork. When I saw it standing on the mantle over the fireplace of her living room, I was really taken aback. It was a wire sculpture. Ian said it had been made with one long piece of wire. Even though it was a bit abstract, it did resemble me a lot. The woman's hair was curly, like mine, and it was the same style that my hair was in when I was with Ian. The woman had large breasts and full thighs, like me. After looking at the sculpture for a while, I realized that I was standing in front of another sign that our relationship was meant to happen. He had received an image of me as I had of him, many years before we had actually met. It brought back to me the thought that there was something that Ian and I were meant to do. After seeing the sculpture, I was rededicated to him and the work.

    Before we left for Mexico, Ian decided that he wanted me to handle all the money. I put all of our money into my checking account and was going to use my debit card to dispense all of our funds. I did not like being in that position. I was used to the men in my life handling the money affairs. I had just gotten a new type of debit card from the bank. It had the Visa logo on it, so it could be used like a credit card. The man at the bank told me that I could use it to pay for everything. I didn't need to carry around a lot of cash. It sounded good. We were ready to go.

WE ARRIVED IN THE YUCATAN IN THE BEGINNING OF September of 1998. When I got out of the plane, I felt like I had been shoved into a wall of hot humidity. This wall had substance and was pressing up against my lungs. I had been used to heat, living in Phoenix, but this was something else. It was hard to breathe. But after a few hours, I started to get used to it. A taxi took us right to the hotel in the middle of Merida. I had been in Merida many years before, but where we ended up did not seem familiar to me.

We went down a long corridor of a street. All the streets in that part of town definitely had the resemblance of old, colonial Merida. The Spanish influence in the architecture was very apparent. All the homes that lined the streets had tall, wooden doors. All the windows had artistic wrought iron bars on them. The houses were painted with bright colors, and they were kept up well.

The hotel that we were dropped off at was old but looked well preserved. It was just like the rest of the buildings in that part of town. We had arranged to stay in the same hotel where Drunvalo Melchizedek was teaching his workshop. The lobby was pleasant, but once we got into our room, we could see the truth about the hotel: it was old and inefficient. When we went to take a shower, we found that there was no hot water. We were able to find some other Americans in nearby rooms. These were people who were taking the workshop with Drunvalo. We were informed that there was only hot water in the morning. After a bit, we went down to the dining room. The dining room was pleasant enough and very proper with tablecloths and cloth napkins. As nice as the restaurant looked, it was lacking in menu options.

After dinner, we went to the pool and talked with some of the class attendees. It was a very relaxed atmosphere. Everyone had their umbrella drinks and some were floating around in the pool in inner tubes. I met some people that I had known from Drunvalo's classes.

I had actually e-mailed some of the people that were by the pool. They had e-mailed me for various reasons. Some had questions about the Flower of Life workshop. Drunvalo wanted people to take the FOL workshop first before they came to one of his workshops. It was nice to actually see them in the flesh. One of the main topics of discussion was currency. This was good, because it gave me a clear picture of what our dollars were worth and what to expect from our exchanges.

Ian had a great time around the pool. He sold a bit of his jewelry. We were talking until we both started yawning. We felt it was time to go to our room. Before we retired, Ian wanted to make sure that we would be able to have breakfast with Drunvalo. I was feeling another airport experience coming on, but at least I would not have to do all the talking this time. We had to make special arrangements to have breakfast with Drunvalo's group. After a bit of finagling, we worked it out.

It was important for Ian to meet Drunvalo. He was religious in his practice of the Merkaba meditation. He kept me faithful with the practice. He felt that Drunvalo was one of the people on the planet that was helping the world get ready for many earth changes. Therefore, meeting Drunvalo was second on his list of people he wanted to meet on the trip.

WHEN WE WENT DOWN TO BREAKFAST, THE SCENE WAS set perfectly. Drunvalo had just sat down at a breakfast table, and there were some empty seats next to him. Without having to be pushed or nudged by Ian, I quickly ran over to the seats and sat down next to Drunvalo. He was a bit surprised to see me. He must have been shocked at my presence there. Before Drunvalo could come up with any answers to these questions that appeared to be racing through his mind, Ian sat down next to me and started to engage him in conversation.

That was my cue to go to the buffet to get some fruit and granola. Meanwhile Ian moved over next to Drunvalo and started to make a fool of himself. Ian was a bit flustered and couldn't get his words out. I looked back from the buffet and chuckled to myself. Ian tongue-tied? Now that was one for the record books. Ian had gotten a chance to talk to a man who was one of his idols.

After Ian could talk without stuttering, he explained a bit of why we were there. When I came back with my full plate, Drunvalo got a break from Ian and started to talk to me. It was nice to see him again. Ian now took his turn at the breakfast buffet. "Is that your boyfriend?" he asked with a tone of disbelief. I nodded in the affirmative. I don't know if Drunvalo was astounded at the thought of me being with such a peculiar man, or if he was just curious. He just looked at me with big eyes after that. The three of us ate and chatted. It was an extremely entertaining breakfast.

After breakfast, Drunvalo escaped from the dining room where Ian had held him prisoner, and we started looking into bus trips. We found out that we could not go to Chichen Itza, as I had hoped. I had never been there, so I wanted to go. Instead, we were able to get a bus to Uxmal and Kabah. I had been to Uxmal many years ago and so I was not too thrilled about a return trip. Yet we were going somewhere, so that was all that really mattered.

We got on the bus and sailed through a green canopy of trees for a couple of hours. I loved the rainforests of Mexico. As we glided along the road I was fascinated by this gigantic, primordial growth kitchen. For thousands of years, Mother Nature has been cooking up a lot of remarkable plants, trees, foods and healing herbs right there. I was also sad to see that so much of the forest had been cleared away.

After a few hours we arrived at Uxmal. When we started into the ruins of Uxmal, I was dumbfounded. I was at the same ruins 25 years ago. When I had visited there the first time, in the 1970's, only one building was visible. My girlfriend and I spent about thirty minutes there. We climbed up the one pyramid that was there, and then we left.

When I returned this time with Ian, I was flabbergasted. There were so many buildings that were uncovered this time. For me, it was like seeing a completely new place. The one temple that I saw back then had been surrounded by trees. The jungle had been so dense, my friend and I did not even think anything else was there at all. I guess the clearing of the rainforests had its good and bad points. If this had not been cleared away, I would not be seeing this magnificent, sprawling ruin. I was fascinated as I walked around.

Uxmal was a prestigious religious center during the time of the Maya. Along with Chichen Itza, it became a dominating force in Mayan culture. The city was founded by a royal family called the Xiu family in 500 A. D. Uxmal was a busy center even up to the time of Cortez. The Xiu family became allies with Cortez in his conquest of the Yucatan. For this reason, the city was not demolished, but spared Spanish domination. The city had been well preserved. It is a fine example of the Mayan skill in architecture.

We spent most of the day wandering around this impressive complex. There was a building called the Governor's Palace. The pyramid that I climbed thirty years ago is called the Pyramid of the Magician. Uxmal also has a handball court. In the Mayan culture, the handball court was used for many important ceremonial reasons. It was much more than a game. The court was often used to settle differences with warring tribes. The losing team was usually sacrificed. I was fortunate to be able to return to this ruin and see everything that I had missed all those years ago.

After a charming meal at the local restaurant, it was time to go to Kabah. We walked the raised roadway to this nearby ruin that was about a quarter of a mile from Uxmal. This was a much smaller cluster of buildings. All of the buildings at the site were dedicated to the rain god, Chaac. The main building was very ornate. It had a whole wall of faces of the rain god carved out of stone. We finished walking this ruin, and then it was time to get back to the bus.

That night we stayed out by the pool again for a while. We talked to our new friends and Ian got to expound on Mayan astrology. We were both happy.

THE NEXT DAY WE WERE ON OUR WAY TO CANCUN VERY early. We were able to find a nice, cheap, little hotel near the beach. It did have hot water all the time, so it was really an upgrade from our hotel with the prestigious exterior. The next morning we took another bus ride. This time we went to Tulum. As the bus sped through the road in the jungle, I could see that there was much more rainforest there. There had not been the hacking of the trees that I saw when we were going to Uxmal. The rainforest was left basically untouched.

It was scorching hot when we got off the bus at Tulum. We were eager to get to the coolness of the ocean. We decided to cool off in the water before exploring the ruins. It was a bit of a walk from where the bus left us, but when we arrived, it was all worth it.

When we reached the water, I took my sarong and hat off and plunged into the ocean. I was delighted to be in the water. The buildings and the sand were sun bleached white. The ocean around Tulum is a luscious, vivid turquoise color. The Caribbean blue waters created an incredible contrast next to the white sand and buildings. I sat and marveled at the color of the ocean for a long time. Ian had a great time frolicking in the water and flirting with the bikini clad women who wandered by.

Finally, it was a bit cooler, and we realized we needed to start exploring the rest of the site. The ruins were in very good shape, compared to many I had seen. There were many structures there. There was a lot of artwork still in place. Before we arrived, Ian had told me that Tulum was the major site for viewing the descending god. He was eager to see the descending god carvings up close. The diving god, as it is also called, represents the myth of Quetzalcoatl and the cycle of

Venus. The legend of Quetzalcoatl tells of a man who was made king of the Maya. He was conceived by virgin birth. He fell into demise and participated in many of the taboos of his culture. After he realized his errors, he committed suicide as he sailed off into the ocean on a boat that was set afire. The gods of the Maya forgave him and resurrected him. He returned to the Maya on a boat from the ocean.

The changes in the cycle of the planet Venus represent the changes in Quetzalcoatl. As the morning star, Venus represents immaturity and impulsiveness to the Maya. During the cycle of Venus, the planet disappears from view. When Venus returns as the evening star, it represents the wisdom and transformation of Quetzalcoatl.

The sculpture in the temples and on the facades of the buildings seemed to make a deep impression on Ian. He sensed his connection to the diving god and started some new jewelry pieces of the descending god when we got home.

Tulum was the jewel of Mayan coastal cities. Like any precious jewel, it had to be guarded. Tulum had one of the greatest defense systems in the Mayan kingdom. The great wall, which has now collapsed, was the focal point of their defenses. It had watchtowers that could detect any invasion by land or sea.

Tulum was a busy seaport for many centuries. There are artifacts at Tulum that come from many different parts of Mexico. Tulum is known to have a great deal of Obsidian. This was brought to the city from great distances. I found that to be very interesting, since my Mayan astrology day lord is Obsidian Blade. Many Obsidian blades made their way through Tulum to the rest of the Mayan empire.

We had a terrific afternoon. We both became absorbed in our visions of the past. That happens to me when I go to an ancient place. We explored the ruins, for the most part, in silence. We were both engrossed in our thoughts.

In the evening, we returned to the hotel. After a great dinner in an open, seaside cafe, we collapsed into each other's warm bodies that had been baking in the sun all day.

OUR PLAN FOR THE NEXT TWO DAYS WAS TO SPEND TIME sightseeing in Cancun. We had three days to wait until our trip by air to Guatemala and our meeting with Don Alejandro. Ian and I were both a bit tired. We just wanted to take it easy and enjoy the ocean. We had to find a place that would accept my debit/credit card. We checked into a Holiday Inn hotel that was right on the beach. It was a state of the art, modern hotel. We thought there would not be a problem using the card there. We went up to our room, enjoyed the view and a few beers.

The next day, it was time to start using the new debit/credit card. We were going to take a bus ride to a water park in the area, which was a bit north of Cancun. When I went to pay for our tickets at the hotel concierge, I received a shock that put a dark cloud over the rest of our trip. My card was rejected! I knew that there was plenty of money in the account, but again I hadn't taken into consideration that there might be a problem using the card in a foreign country. The debit card with the Visa logo was new. I guess that it was very new in foreign countries. We could not go anywhere. We were stranded.

That started my long series of phone calls to the bank. It was the weekend when I made the first call, so nothing was going to be done. We soon felt like prisoners of the hotel. We could not go out to eat or pay for anything else in Cancun. All that we could do was charge our room and meals in the hotel.

It was unfortunate that we were not able to enjoy ourselves in spite of the crisis. I was overcome by the fear of being stuck in a foreign country without money. Worse yet, we had money and were not able to use it. I had been through financial traumas in Mexico in the past, so I did not want to relive that again. I was feeling a lot of shame that I had not gotten the money particulars under control. All of my poor money management scenarios from the past kept parading across my mind.

I knew that Ian was feeling a tremendous amount of anger. I didn't need to be psychic to figure that out! He had trusted me, and I accidentally made a mess of the situation. I sensed that he could see the whole trip being for nothing. He probably felt that I was going to sabotage his opportunity to see Don Alejandro. All the money and time spent on the trip would be wasted if we did not make it to the interview. That was the most important part of the trip. We hadn't paid for the plane to Guatemala, either. We had to do that when we got to the plane. Remember, the Internet and advanced booking had still not manifested fully in the third world.

Instead of walking around Cancun and enjoying the sights, we both laid in our beds, staring up at the ceiling, suppressing our feelings, saying not even a word to each other. Ian did not even look out the window. I had a few meals in the hotel, but Ian did not eat for those two nerve-racking days.

I had been on the phone six times in two days. The bank said that when Monday came, they would get it straightened out. Ian only drank water. He just stayed in his bed, staring at the ceiling.

MONDAY MORNING ARRIVED, AND WE HAD TO GET MONEY out of the bank. We needed to pay our hotel bill, pay for a taxi ride to the airport, as well as the plane that would take us down to Guatemala City. If we could not get on that plane, Ian would have lost another chance to meet with Don Alejandro. A lot was riding on my ability to get the money out of the bank.

I was up at 5 a.m. that morning. Ian and I packed our bags and were affirming that we were going to Guatemala. I had been told by the bank that I needed to go to an ATM that morning that was located on another street, behind the hotel. I was told that I should be able to get the funds there. That was still a big question mark. I had gone to the ATM in the hotel and had been turned down for cash. While it was still dark, I walked out of the hotel and down an alley to the ATM. The streets were empty. I felt unsafe walking by myself in a deserted area of any Mexican town, especially one like Cancun. Ian was not being his usual helpful self. He was angry and did not even want to look at me. He would not walk with me to the ATM. He wanted to stay in the room. I had to make the journey myself.

On my walk to the ATM, I saw a taxicab and a driver. I went up to him and he told me in English, where to go. I felt better knowing that he was there. He told me that he would be there when I got back, and not to worry. I felt better about going through the darkness and the ally, knowing that I was within yelling distance of someone else.

I followed his directions and found the ATM. Holding my breath; I put my card in and punched in the numbers. I asked for the maximum that I could get in one day, which was $300 USD or $600 Pesos. That would be enough to pay the hotel bill and pay for our flight to Guatemala City. I had never felt more blessed than when I saw those bills start to come out of the machine. Thank you guides, teacher, angels, whomever else for helping me! The cab driver was not there when I came back through the alleyways from the ATM. Now I was terrified to be walking alone with so much cash!

The sun was beginning to come up, and there were more people on the streets. I ran back to the hotel, paid the bill at the front desk and called to the room. "Get our stuff and get down here. We have a plane to catch."

In less than ten minutes, Ian was in the lobby with our luggage, ready to go. When he came downstairs with our bags, he did not smile. No peck on the cheek, no nothing. We got in the taxi that took us to the Cancun airport. We paid for our tickets and literally ran to catch the plane. When we found two seats in the back and landed our hineys in them, I finally started to relax. I knew, as I was watching the buildings on the ground get smaller, that we would be able to make the appointment.

IAN HAD ARRANGED FOR THIS FLIGHT TO GUATEMALA City. He calculated that we would have just enough time to take a taxi to the address, which we had been told was Don Alejandro's house in the city. We ran from the plane to the next taxi. Once the bags were secure in the taxi, we ambled our way toward the city.

Guatemala City was like any other large Hispanic city: dirty, smelly and crowded. Old cars and even older buses navigated slowly through the sea of traffic. There were a great many street venders who would hold up strange foods to the taxi windows, in case we wanted to have something bizarre to eat. Many items were held up to the windows: clothes, colorful bark paintings, iguanas, etc. It was sad and amusing all at the same time.

After about twenty minutes of slowly making our way through the gnarled, congested streets, we started to get out of the commercial area and into the residential area. It was still as crowded, but somehow it seemed nicer. The houses looked like they were well kept. As we slowly drove by the houses, I could see iron bars that protected courtyards with gardens and laundry hanging up to dry. There were many kids and dogs chasing each other around inside these bared courtyards. These streets had a neighborhood feel to them. The taxi stopped in front of a house that had an iron fence and was painted Cerulean blue. I could see some well-manicured trees and bushes inside. Don Alejandro's home looked very pleasant. It was obvious that there was enough money to maintain the house properly.

We rang a bell, and a familiar man came out to greet us. He had been with Don Alejandro at the airport in Santa Fe. We recognized each other. He smiled, nodded his head and let us through the gate. We were taken to a small room located in the front of the house. It had the feeling of a sitting room or parlor. Benches and chairs lined the walls of the room. There were pictures on the wall and lace doilies on the tables. It looked like a very neat and clean rendition of many of the Mexican living rooms I had seen in the past in Mexico. We waited for about ten minutes before the esteemed day keeper we had chased down at the airport came in through a side door. Ian let out a gigantic sigh when he saw Don Alejandro. Ian smiled and looked very proud as he shook Don Alejandro's hand. I shook everyone's hand as well. Then we all sat down and got down to business.

I was extremely grateful that the bodyguard was acting as the interpreter. Since I had returned to Mexico, I had become painfully aware that my Spanish was a bit rusty. It had been 25 years since I had spoken much Spanish. I did all right when I had to speak, but I was not even close to sounding well-expressed. I just got the job done with no frills. Hispanics, however, love their language with its many frills. They like to express themselves in an flamboyant manner. It is part of what I call the Hispanic ardor of the heart that comes through in their speech. I was glad that I did not have the responsibility of translating at such an important meeting. I just got to sit back and observe. What happened next will never leave my memory. It was a profound event.

Ian started to talk to Don Alejandro. The bodyguard stopped Ian and said that Don Alejandro knew why he was there. Don Alejandro wanted Ian to explain why he was there. He wanted the whole story. Ian went into a long speech on what he had discovered. Ian started off by telling Don Alejandro that he had been studying Mayan astrology for a long time. Ian sought to make the wisdom of Mayan astrology available to the general public. He wanted to share the guidance that the Tzolkin brings to the rest of the world. He had a desire to help people use Mayan astrology to improve their lives and be in harmony with the Earth Mother and the Galactic Center of the Milky Way. He said that most of all, he wanted to bring the truth and the accurate count of the Tzolkin to the public. His desire was that the people of the earth have the count of the Tzolkin that the Kiché Maya have preserved for centuries.

Ian explained that the Tzolkin had already spread all over the world, and people were using it incorrectly. Ian wanted to bring Don Alejandro's count of the calendar to the world. His dream was to have the count that the ancient Maya used for the sacred calendar dispersed to all humanity. He felt that the Tzolkin could bring harmony to our planet. It would align people with Hu'nab Ku, the center of the galaxy, as it had the ancient Maya. It would help people know how to use the energy of each day in a way that would be the best for them and all of humanity.

Ian went on to say that his charts or method for connecting with the energy of the day was very simple. Anyone could use it. Anyone could easily find out who they are and how to be in harmony with the energy of the day.

Ian could be the most eloquent of speakers. He did have an incredible way with words when he focused. He was focusing that day. The sweat was dripping down his neck. The bodyguard seemed to appreciate what Ian was saying.

I could understand what the bodyguard was saying and I felt good about what was being translated for Don Alejandro. The three men were beginning to have what I could only describe in Spanish as *simpatico* for each other. They were beginning to resonate with each other, understand each other and feel good about each other.

After about ten minutes, Don Alejandro began to speak. I could tell that he had been thinking about what Ian had been saying and he now wanted to do some teaching.

"We have been able to keep track of the days for a long time," said Don Alejandro. "This has been our job. We are proud to take the knowledge and share it with others. But it is important that the day be correct. It is important for our whole lives that we are on the right day of the calendar. It is more than a calendar to us; it is the core of our culture, our knowledge and our present day life. If we were to lose the calendar, we would lose our world."

I had never heard Don Alejandro speak before. He was very expressive. I knew then that I was in the presence of a very learned and wise man. I now knew why Claudia was so devoted to him.

Then Don Alejandro started to talk about the day. "Today is 12 IK or 12 Wind" Having thought that my day lord was Wind for a while, I had some understanding about that day lord and number. "It is a good to talk and to communicate this day. It can be very beneficial to talk and share on this day. Today communication will bring understanding. That is why we are talking to you today," said Don Alejandro.

At this point, Ian decided to interject. He asked Don Alejandro and the bodyguard to use the chart. He patiently walked them through the steps that were necessary to figure out what day it was on his charts. The bodyguard was accurately translating everything that Ian was saying. He also seemed to be interested in Ian's creation. The three men were hunched over, looking at the charts in a very solemn way. Don Alejandro could see, even before the end result had been achieved, that it was not complicated. Then, all three men, at the same time, looked up at each other and said "*Doce* (12) IK!"

I could see those grey lightning bolts coming out around Ian and Don Alejandro's heads. Don Alejandro was in high spirits. Ian was elated. We were all exuberant. The energy in the room had become one of jubilation. All three men sat back in their chairs and had big smiles on their faces. It was important to all of them. I knew that Ian felt he had succeeded. Ian had hit a home run and was now basking in the glory of slowly walking to home plate, with the crowds cheering.

What a glorious moment it was! I could see the little lightning bolts filling the room. I too was ecstatic. Ian had completed his objective. He had done what he had set out to do. He had made Don Alejandro smile. For the next 15 minutes or so, the men were shaking hands, smiling and being very enthusiastic. At the end Ian asked Don Alejandro if he had his blessing for the project. The reply was immediate and positive. Don Alejandro was happy. Don Alejandro's head was bobbling up and down and he was saying "*Si, si, si.*"

It appeared that Don Alejandro was pleased with Ian's invention. He saw that this would help his own people learn more about the Tzolkin. It would help all people who were interested to use the calendar without difficulty. Ian gave Don Alejandro the charts. Then it was time for us to go. There was a lot of hand waving and smiling as we left the house. I felt for a moment that we were Japanese people, for all the bowing and smiling that was going on. Another taxi was there to take us to our destination for the evening. I could officially say that the audience with Don Alejandro was a success and Ian had finally achieved this goal.

IT WAS A SPECTACULAR DAY. IAN WAS IN A EUPHORIC state. He was finally smiling. We got in the taxi and he told the driver the name of a place where we were going to spend the night. In the taxi, Ian started to break down. He started sobbing. I moved near him to comfort him and put my arms around him. It was the first time he had let me touch him in three days. He had been on the edge of trauma for days, so it was nice to see him finally start to unwind.

Ian knew where we were going, but I had no idea. We only went a short way in the taxi. We ended up at a little town that was near the active volcano, Pacaya. When we got out of the Taxi, I felt that we had finally gotten to Guatemala. We were right in the middle of the market place. Now I was beginning to feel something familiar. I realized that Guatemala was like Mexico used to be twenty-five years ago.

I had been very disappointed when we went to Mexico because the Mexican people did not wear their traditional dress anymore. The Mexicans seemed to be completely Americanized. They had lost themselves in trying to be like us. They were so obsessed with all things American; they were throwing away who they really are. The only people that dressed in traditional clothing were those who were performing for the tourists. I hope that at some point they will be able to get back in touch with their heritage.

It was beautiful to see the Guatemalan people in motion. There were men and the women selling their goods and walking with their families dressed in their traditional clothing. I have to say that when I arrived there that day, and after I had walked around a bit and saw how the people conducted themselves, I felt very proud of the Guatemalans. Not only was I proud of them, but I could see that they were proud of themselves. Their self-respect was reflected in their attire. I am not going to say that the streets were as clean as the streets in Switzerland, but I will say that good self-esteem was reflected in their environment.

Almost all the women were dressed neatly, and their hair was combed and braided with ribbons. I felt like I was in the middle of a walking art gallery. It was not a market day. It was just a regular day. The combinations of colors, textures and fabrics were intoxicating.

While I was enchanted by the fabric art, Ian just wanted to find a place to stay for the night. He was emotionally depleted. He needed to lay his tired bones down soon. We found a decent and reasonably-priced place to stay. We left our luggage in our room and went across the street to get something to eat.

Across the street from our hotel was a quaint rooftop restaurant. We went upstairs and had a great view of the city. Then a woman, who was dressed impeccably in a blouse of embroidered flowers and a skirt of many shades of midnight blue, approached our table and took our order. We had our victory feast of steak, beans, rice, tortillas and several beers. The sun was setting while we were eating, and it was a grand conclusion to a monumental day. Of course, Ian could only talk about the meeting. Over and over he repeated the words Don Alejandro had said. "12 IK, we got the same day, 12 IK!" He said as we toasted to the day again and again.

I did not grow tired of hearing him talk that night. It was his right. He had earned it. He had suffered greatly to get to this day. He had traveled thousands of miles to have this day, and I was not going to take one moment away from him. I did not interject a word. I smiled, laughed and nodded my head. I loved to see his blue eyes flash. His eyes were full of the bitter sweetness of a victory that had been achieved after a long struggle.

The place that we were staying in did have a shower in the room. I was thankful for that. It did not have much privacy, though. The walls looked like they were made out of rice paper. But we didn't care. Ian just took off his clothes and went right to sleep. That night I dreamed about a black raven.

The raven was flying toward me with a big worm in its beak. I opened my mouth and the raven dropped the worm in it. Even though this would have totally nauseated me in real life, in the dream, it was superb. In the dream I felt that I needed to follow the raven. I started running after the bird, asking it to come back. I ran over a hill, following the raven and we disappeared from view.

WE ONLY HAD ONE DAY IN THIS TOWN BEFORE WE HAD TO head back to Mexico. This disappointed me terribly. I loved it there. We took a walk away from the market toward the plaza. The first order of business was to get more money.
We had been told about a place where we would not have any problem getting some money. The town was very busy this time of day. We found the place that was the money exchange and telegraph office all in one. This place seemed to be equipped to handle our needs. It only took a few minutes for us to get the money we needed. The banking system seemed to be working well for us now.

With some cash in our hands, we were ready to get some breakfast. A few doors away from the money office, was a sweet little café. It was painted a pale apricot color and was very neat and clean. All the tables had glass tops and the chairs were wood with woven straw seats and backs. We had a pleasant breakfast and then decided to explore the town.

It was a terrific day for us. Ian and I looked at all the colorful and fascinating vendor stands, even though he felt that we did not have any money to buy anything. He was being very strict with me. It was clear that he still did not totally forgive me for all the grief I had caused him. Now that is hell for a woman. All these fantastic clothes to buy and not allowed to spend money! I did not mind his restrictions. I was too elated to be upset by anything.

THAT EVENING WE RECONNECTED EMOTIONALLY WITH a night of ardent love making that earned us a lot of nasty looks as we checked out of the hotel the following morning. We were going to catch a bus into Mexico that morning. It was going to be a long bus ride to our next destination, which was Mexico City. It would take us two days. Ian had made this trip before. We would go to the Guatemala/ Mexico border that night and go on to Mexico City the following day. Once we arrived in Mexico City, we would take another bus to our final destination, Tepoztlan.

We started our journey at mid-morning. When we entered the bus, we knew right away that we were going into a different life arena. We were the only non-Hispanic travelers on the bus. This was the "real people's" bus. They were the farmers and the poor. Even though they were poor, they were dressed well and they looked fresh and neat.

We found a little corner at the back of the bus and settled in for the journey. A great deal of food was being exchanged on this bus ride. All the passengers seemed to have enough food handy for themselves and several others. In the beginning of the trip there were people who would get on the bus to sell the travelers food, and then get off the bus at the next stop. The catering came to you. There were always a few rest stops that also had restaurants at them. We had decided to eat there. We didn't want to take a chance on getting sick, not on a bus ride like this.

The bus driver and his assistant were at the front of the bus. The assistant was there to help the bus driver get out of tight spots when backing up or parking. The assistant had a woman and a child with him. Her traditional clothing was marvelous and her hair was entwined with many colored ribbons. Her little girl was also dressed neatly in a precious little Guatemalan dress. The mother and daughter seemed to be very happy to be with the man who did the yelling and slapping of the bus as it maneuvered out of the bus station.

After rigorously looking us over for about a half hour, the other travelers went back to their talking and various stages of food consumption. I must say that traveling by bus was a great way to see the countryside. The bus was going higher and higher into the mountains. It was a striking landscape. The land was a patchwork quilt of different shades of green. The rainy season was nurturing the earth so that the crops would be strong and abundant. We passed countless fields of corn that were almost ready to harvest.

As nightfall came upon us, we were getting close to the Guatemalan border. It was also beginning to rain. As we got closer to the border, the tension built for us. All of the money that we had was in the Guatemalan currency, the Quetzal.

Ian knew that we had to find someone at the border that would change our money into Mexican Pesos. Ian had talked about it a lot on the bus. We had found out what the exchange rate was before we left. We knew what the money was worth. The trick was to find a person who would give a fair exchange rate for our money. A little bit of theft was normal, but we did not want to be completely taken. This was something that we were going to have to do together. I would be the mouthpiece in this transaction and spindly Ian was going to be the muscle and protect our money. We knew that we were in a situation that could be volatile.

As we got to the border, the rain was pouring down, and the bus came to a stop. We all filed out. Most of us went to the only restaurant that was in sight. Once we got inside, I knew that this was an authentic Guatemalan diner. The place was also spick and span. It passed my cleanliness test. We sat down at a table with plastic tablecloths and metal chairs. There were three choices for dinner. We got the one with the chicken. It was a satisfying, plentiful meal.

As the night wore on, a heartrending scene unfolded. The men were beginning to get drunk. The assistant, with the woman and child were sitting near us. The assistant was getting drunker and drunker. He started to wave his arms around in large gestures and talk very loudly and slowly. The woman with the child that was with him was beginning to look panicked. She did not like what was happening. I felt that she had gone through this before. She was keeping an ever-present vigil and had to grab him many times to save him from falling off of his chair.

As we exited the restaurant, the rain was hammering down upon the miniscule border rest stop. It wasn't a cold rain, but it was a heavy one. This was very common during this time of year. It was a time when the crops got their last big downpours from a nurturing sky to help them grow to their paramount.

It was time to find a place to sleep for the night. Ian knew exactly where to go. It was the only place to go. It was right next door. As we walked over to the lodging place, we saw the bus driver's assistant, the woman and the child, huddled together in the street, getting the full brunt of the rain upon them. The three of them were covered with some plastic. Their heads were soaking wet. The woman looked up at me with eyes filled with misery. Her man was drunk and snoring, next to her. Her child was asleep in her arms. This is where they were spending the night.

I wished I could do something for them. Ian pulled me away from them before I could think of anything to do. We went into what was too strange to be called a hotel. It was $100 Quetzals to have a room to sleep in for the night. (That was about $15 USD.) We were sleeping in the penthouse accommodations. There were men sleeping on cots that were lined up in the entrance area. We made our way, through rows of snoring men, to the back, where the private rooms were. We actually had a room where we could close the door.

After we got into our room, Ian closed the door and told me what was going to happen. "When the lights go out, all the roaches are going to come out and they will be crawling all over you."

I think that my eyes were close to bulging out of my head. Even though he issued no reaction, I knew that he was enjoying watching me freak out. A long tiring bus ride, and now you want me to sleep with roaches crawling all over me all night?

"Then we are not going to turn off the light!" That was my final statement. He said nothing, but kept the light on. I guess it was better than hearing me scream all night as the bugs paraded over me.

"Across the way is the bathroom and shower. It is a communal bathroom. There are several stalls and showers there," Ian explained. My eyes were really bulging out of my head now. Now, if I wanted to use the bathroom, one of the snoring men in the hallway might come in! I was in the middle of Cockroach Hell! Or was this just a weird Indiana Jones movie? I had been used to roughing it when I lived in Mexico, but this was unlike any place I had ever stayed in Latin America. I was having an experience of the real people, all right.

After giving me abundant hugs while I sat on my piece of wood that doubled as a bed, he went to his "bed." It was also a piece of wood with a cloth over it and a pillow. He got under his cover, pulled it over his face, and became still. I am sure he was laughing himself to sleep, as he turned away from me. I guess he slept that night. I did not hear any sounds or movement coming from his side of the room. I ought to know, I was up all night. I found myself going to the bathroom several times that night, filled with dread that a snoring man might awaken and find me in there. I was a wreck when the morning came.

I GUESS IAN DID SLEEP, BECAUSE HE SEEMED TO BE IN better shape than I was. He was all fresh and perky! We got up, and dragging my bags behind me, we went to the area where we were going to change our money.

The money changing went fairly easily. We got a decent price for our Quetzals. With a fist full of Pesos, we went to the bus area to get two tickets to Mexico City. We entered a bus that also did not have any non-Hispanics on it, but I was used to that by this time. I had realized that no Americans or foreigners in their right mind would travel like this. We went to our comfort zone in the back, and I felt safe there.

This bus ride was to take us through the middle of Southern Mexico. We were going into the highlands of Mexico, which had also been the home of the ancient Maya.

This was to be an overnight bus ride. We would stay on the same bus until we got to Mexico City the next morning.

The journey during the day was uneventful. I appreciated seeing the cornfields and the mountains that day. It had only been about two hours after dark when the bus pulled over to the side of the road and stopped. As the bus was coming to a stop, I could see brutes with guns standing outside waiting for us. If I wasn't scared out of my skin before, I certainly was now! When the bus was stopped, two men with rifles entered the bus. They started walking slowly down the aisles. As they were coming closer, they looked at certain travelers and asked them to get off the bus. About six people were standing outside when they came to us. Ian had told me to have my passport in my hand to show it to them. When a man who was about 5' 3" 200 lbs., with short hair and a mustache came up to us, Ian handed him our passports. I am glad that Ian was handling it. My hands probably would have been shaking. The man looked at our passports, returned them, and turned and walked back to the front of the bus.

In about an hour, we came to a bus stop that had a restaurant and restroom. I ran into the restroom and ran back to the bus. I had to pass by a group of men with big guns to get to the restroom. It was not clear to me if these men were soldiers or just gun happy Mexicans. They were not wearing any type of uniforms.

Thank God I was with a man, even if he was not really big and burly. Ian's presence was helping me to get through this situation. I would have come unglued if I had been alone.

After the bus started moving, I began to relax. At times like this, I just had to roll myself into fetal ball and put as much of my body as I could next to Ian. He chuckled when I did that. Like "Oh, how cute, Abby is scared."

As the bus worked its way toward Mexico City, at a speed that was nowhere fast enough for me, I felt my body calming down. I just allowed the hum of the bus motor to lull me to sleep. My eyes had not been closed very long, maybe an hour, when the bus was starting to come to a stop again. I sat up and looked around and sure enough, there were the apelike men with the guns again. We had arrived at another stop and went through another flashing of the passports. I was finally getting used to it.

It was about 2 a. m. in the morning, when we came to a stop again. Ian had our passports handy, so the men could see them. This time, however, when the men came walking down the aisle, they started asking people to get out of the bus, as they had at the first stop. This did not feel good to me. They picked certain people here and there, seemingly at random, to get off the bus. They came to us and asked us to get off too.

I was not happy! I tried to hide the terror in my eyes, by looking down. They made us all stand in a line. The guards came walking down the line and then talked to a few people. The people were speaking Spanish very quickly. I could not understand anything that was being said. Then one of the men with a gun came to a pretty, young woman who was dressed a bit flashy. She had on a shirt that had sequins. There was little light there, just a few street lights in the distance. Just enough light to see the sequins flash as she moved. The guard/soldier/I don't know what, started to yell at the woman. He kept yelling at her for about five minutes. Then he started shaking her. When he stopped, she was in tears. FINALLY, he let her go and moved on to the next person. Was she being punished for wearing sequins? That experience was only two people away from Ian and me.

"Oh, for joy, I can't wait until you get to us." I have to say that Ian just stood there and took a strong posture. The man started to examine our passports. I thought to myself "I know you can't read English, so what is the deal?"

He pretended that he was studying them thoroughly. He could probably read the dates and see the stamps. He did this to both of our passports, his eyes looking back and forth between the passports and us. Finally he gave us back our passports and let us all get back on the bus. We were silent for the rest of the night. We had two more inspection stops that night. Thankfully, we did not have to get out of the bus again. Ian stayed in the bus until we reached a large town in the morning. After my second sleepless night, we arrived in Mexico City in the afternoon.

THE HOTEL THAT WE STAYED IN THAT NIGHT WAS a phenomenal contrast between where we had slept for the last two nights. When we arrived at the hotel, it was clear that we had just entered another world. It was the world of elegant, modern accommodations. There was hot water, clean beds, room service and an impressive view of the round-about called the Plaza de Belles Arêtes in the middle of Mexico City. Ian had booked a room in this hotel before we went on the trip. We would stay in this luxurious hotel for the night and then go on to Tepoztlan the next morning on a bus. Oh NO!

After we changed our clothes, we went out and had a terrific dinner. It was completely the opposite of the dinner that we had at the Guatemalan border. Now we were eating amidst waiters in tuxedos, linen tablecloths, linen napkins, and delicious Americanized food. My comfort zone had been restored and something inside of me was screaming with happiness.

That night I slept in Ian's arms. I did not like to sleep that way. Usually, I would have kissed him goodnight and turned away. Not that night. I lay in his embrace and did not move all night.

THE NEXT MORNING, WE TOOK THE LAST OF OUR busses to get to Tepoztlan. This was a very different experience than our last bus ride. The bus had a big Mercedes logo on the front of it. It was the Cadillac of busses. It had great seats. Coffee and snacks were being served in the back of the bus that was included in the fare. This was a very popular bus route. There were a few men with guns at the terminal, at the beginning of the ride. They seemed to be stationary and there to observe. We had gotten enough money in Mexico City to last us a few days. There were no problems getting the money from the machine now. Everything was going great. I was in familiar territory now.

When we arrived in Cuernavaca, we could have waited for a bus, but we wanted to get to Tepoztlan ASAP. We went over to a group of taxis that were hovering near the bus station. We found one taxi driver that spoke a little English. Ian had never been to Pablo's place. All we knew about it was that it was called El Portal. Ian said that it was in a little town called Amatlan, which was like a suburb of Tepoztlan. When I had come to Tepoztlan all those years ago, I did not remember a little town called Amatlan. I was to find out that much had changed in Tepoztlan.

When we arrived at Tepoztlan, I found it astonishing that the town had become so big. I recognized the plaza, but so much had been built around it. There were now double the stores and buildings around the plaza. It was great to be back. Nothing that I remembered of the stores and the town was the same. There was a big stage in one part of the main plaza. I assumed that was for public celebrations.

As we drove into town, I could see that there were banners up everywhere. They were announcing the 16th of September. That was Mexican Independence day. I surmised that the town was going to have a big party. I was looking forward to finding El Portal, the fiesta and staying there. I had experienced enough adventure for a while.

The taxi driver did not know where El Portal was. He did not even know where Amatlan was. Our taxi driver was very energetic and wanted to do a good job of getting us to our location. We told him all that we knew about the place. In the plaza of Tepoztlan he started asking people where the place called El Portal was located. No one knew. We kept seeing one shaking head after another responding "NO" to the question.

Then Ian told the taxi driver to ask people where Amatlan was. The first woman the taxi driver asked pointed down the street we were on. We were making a bit of progress. We headed out of town and knew that we were going in the right direction. After we had gotten out of the main part of town, our taxi driver started hanging his head out of the window and yelling at people "Amatlan? Amatlan?"

People kept pointing. They indicated that we were going in the right direction, so everything seemed ok. It was starting to get dark, and it was starting to rain. The rain did not make it any easier for us find our way. The road was getting muddy and narrow. Our taxi driver was still yelling Amatlan out the window every time he saw someone on the road. Soon all of the people were out of the rain and inside, so we had no one to guide us. Suddenly we arrived at a little plaza with a sign that said that we were in Amatlan. Now what?

There were four small streets that were leading out of the tiny plaza in different directions. Our taxi driver stopped and found someone to ask for directions. Ian kept saying "El Portal, El Portal" and no one knew what we were talking about. It got to be comical to see Ian standing in the rain, saying to everyone who walked by, "El Portal?" This could have gone on forever, but I decided to get out of the taxi and help. I started to say Pablo, to people, but still had no luck. Then after I said Pablo, el Americano, really loud, a woman pointed to one of the small roads that led out of the plaza. She pointed to a road that was very muddy. The taxi driver was relieved. As we went down the slushy road, the taxi driver was speaking in his broken English and smiling. His smile evaporated when the taxi got stuck in the mud. He stopped the car and got out to look at the situation. Ian got out as well. The taxi driver then took something out of the trunk that came in handy for muddy roads. He put a big piece of plywood in front of the rear wheel, and got back in the taxi. Ian stayed outside to see how things were going. Fortunately, the taxi was able to get out to the muddy pit it had landed in. It was able to continue on down the road. We saw a Mexican man walking in the rain and we started shouting "PABLO" at him. He pointed in the direction that we were going. It was about five more minutes down the road when the road got considerably smaller. The taxi driver was afraid to go to the end of the road, and so were we. Ian and I got out of the taxi and started calling out "PABLO" very loud and in every direction.

After a few yells, we heard "Ian" back. Ian screamed Pablo a few more times, until a short man, who looked Hispanic and had shoulder length white hair, came out from behind a big wall. He ran up to Ian and gave him a big hug. I gave Pablo a big hug too. As Pablo and Ian took our bags out of the taxi, we were all happy, except for the taxi driver. Pablo threw our bags over the big wall. Then he told me that we all had to jump over the wall, as there was no door to the place. Yes, we were at our destination. Yeah, we were safe!

Once over the wall, Ian and Pablo had a long embrace complete with a lot of backslapping. Then Ian introduced me to Pablo. As I listened to him speak English, I could tell that he was from the U. S. He seemed to be very healthy, lively and in good spirits.

When we had jumped over the wall, we landed in the kitchen area. Pablo called the place El Portal. That was really his name for it. None of the locals called it that. Pablo told us he called it El Portal because there was an outline of a door on one of the rock faces. We could not see that at night. He told us that we would be able to see it in the morning. Pablo said that he called it El Portal because he felt that the place was a portal to another world. I really didn't care what the place was called as long as I was safe.

We spent that evening sitting in the kitchen while Pablo and Ian caught up. I could not see much of the rest of the complex. Ian, of course, was bursting with the news about Don Alejandro. Pablo was very interested in Ian's Mayan astrology project.

I guess that my yawning gave Pablo the hint that we were tired and needed to sleep. Pablo led us through the rain, through the compound, to a group of tepees. "A TEPEE! What is this?" The tepees were on wooden platforms. Some of them were occupied. There was candlelight illuminating a couple of them. Pablo led us to one and helped me up the side of the platform. Ian entered the tepee first. When I entered the tepee, I was able to see, by the candle Ian had lit, that there were a bunch of blankets and sleeping bags in one area of the tepee. This was going to be our home for the next few days.

I found it interesting that no water was getting into the tepee while it was raining outside, even though there was the usual hole at the top. The wooden platform that the tepee was mounted on was wet, but the inside was completely dry.

Ian and I divided up the blankets and sleeping bags. Ian went to one side of the tepee and told me that he wanted to be by himself that night. I felt that I was going to sleep a deep dreamless sleep so I could forgo a night of snuggling. I didn't have the desire to find out what was wrong with Ian that night. I thought that in the morning he would be his affectionate self. I did sleep well that night.

IAN HAD ALREADY GOTTEN DRESSED AND WAS OUT OF the tepee when I awoke. When I had gotten dressed and opened the flap of the tepee, I was bowled over by what I saw. Before me was a luxuriant, emerald paradise! I was seeing lush, fertile rainforest terrain. Our encampment was set right in the middle of it. I saw tepees in two rows. There were six, complete with platforms, which lined the little path that we had walked down last night.

It was this little path that interested me. Did it lead to a bathroom?? I got out of the tepee and started down the path. I realized that I could go only one way. The path headed out into the overgrown jungle in the opposite direction. I went in the direction that led to a grouping of buildings.

I soon came to what I will call the bathhouse. This was an area that had showers and toilet stalls. I turned on one of the showers and there was hot water! That was a good sign. I left the bathhouse area and got back on the path, heading away from the tepees.

After walking a bit further, I saw the area where we had first arrived last night. Ian and Pablo were sitting in the kitchen/dining area having coffee. As I walked up, Pablo motioned to the cooking area where there was a coffee pot on the stove and nearby an assortment of fresh fruit. I got some of both and carried a plate and cup over to where the two men were sitting. Pablo was very polite. After he said hello to me, he got back to his conversation with Ian and acted like I was not there.

Suddenly, the reason for Ian's standoffish attitude became clear to me. There was a stunning young Hispanic woman coming our way. She had long straight black hair and big, brown cow eyes. She was dressed in a sarong that was tied at her hip. It had a big slit on the side that showed her exquisite legs when she walked. The rest of her attire consisted of a bathing suit bra top. She walked up to Pablo and gave him a luscious good morning kiss. Then she went over to the juicer and started making juice. When she was done making the juice, she gave Pablo, Ian and me a glass. Then the woman, whose name turned out to be Beatrice, sat down next to Pablo and started to caress his neck and his back.

"Well," I thought, "At least she is taken." Or was she? Maybe she was an El Portal woman, at the disposal of all the male visitors. As it turned out she didn't pay much attention to Ian, so I felt a bit safer. She must have been about 23, and Pablo seemed to be about 55. Then I remembered that a younger woman with older men is the norm in Mexico.

Ian was standoffish in the morning as well. I got the idea that there was to be no lovey-dovey stuff while we were in the presence of Pablo. You expose me to thugs with guns and Cockroach Hell and then you can't be nice to me in public? All I could really do was sit back, drink my mango/papaya juice and see what was going to unfold. At least I was braced for something to happen. Something that would make me feel old and ugly.

After we ate our breakfast, Pablo wanted to take us for a tour of the facility. He wanted to show us El Portal. The four of us left the dining area and started on our tour. We walked toward a great open space that was covered with grass. As we crossed the space, I could see a vague outline of a door on the rock. "Is that why Pablo calls this place El Portal?" I thought. I soon realized that was the portal in question. Pablo went into a lengthy description about why he gave this name to the rock wall. I smiled politely, but I was not interested. I was glad when we moved on to another area of the compound.

At one side of the open, grassy space was a large room on stilts. It could only be entered by climbing up a ladder that appeared to be thirty feet high. That was Pablo's room. It was up on stilts so that he could see what was going on anywhere in the compound. It was also handy to be in a room on stilts when the place flooded during the rainy season. At one side of the rock wall, where the "portal" was located, was an area that had been used for sweat lodges. Next Pablo showed us some other distinctive parts of the property. We walked all the way over to a fence that looked like the split rail fences of the pioneer days. He was able to show us a path that was on the other side of the little fence.

"This is the path that the pilgrims take every year when they go to honor the birthplace of Quetzalcoatl," Pablo said proudly. There had been a legend that Jesus Christ was reborn as Quetzalcoatl right in this very spot. Actually, the spot was up this little path a bit. Mormon pilgrims came to this place every year to honor the transition of the Christ. This was an impressive detail to Ian. It added to his feeling that El Portal was a sacred place. After this disclosure, the grand tour was ended. Pablo told us that he had worked very hard to get the property in good shape.

We made our way back to the eating area. It was really the central location where the visitors congregated when they wanted to lounge around and meet the other visitors. When we returned to the kitchen, there was a short, elderly woman who was making breakfast for us and the other visitors that were beginning to arrive at the eating area. Soon a great looking feast of scrambled eggs, tortillas, beans and hot sauce was being served up by this little woman who looked like a cross between a dwarf and an alien. Even though she looked old, she maneuvered through the kitchen and the breakfast as if she were Beatrice's age.

I also noticed that all the other tepee campers were young. Ian, Pablo and I were the only people there over thirty. "You can look Ian, but please don't do anything weird that would embarrass me." That was the silent prayer that I sent up to God as these gorgeous women were walking around the dining area and smiling at Ian.

Fortunately, all of the gorgeous women seemed to be with gorgeous young men. That was a bit of a relief. The rest of the morning, I was left to myself while Ian and Pablo were going through male bonding. Pablo was a new ear to bend, and he seemed to be delighted with all that Ian had to say.

WHEN IT GOT INTO THE EARLY PART OF THE AFTERNOON, Pablo said that we were going into town. He told me to put on some good shoes for walking and to take a rain covering. The sky was not cloudy, but I knew from living in this part of Mexico, that this was a time when the rains came nearly every day. I actually liked this time of year in Mexico. It was a time when the land was being nurtured. The power of the growth cycle of the rainforest was easy to sense and felt very exhilarating.

I enjoyed the hike into town. The road was muddy, but it was not a problem when you were walking. As we walked along the road, more houses were beginning to come into sight. After about an hour of walking, we began to see the town come into focus. The homes along the road gave way to stores and other types of buildings that went along with a town.

When we got to town, Ian and I went one way, and Pablo and Beatrice went the other. We had to make another bank stop. It was going to be a holiday, so it was best to get money before the holiday began. After a quick stop at the bank, Ian and I were ready to explore the town. Even though I had been there before, the town had grown a lot and was really new to me. The market place had doubled in size and there was a lot more to see, smell and feel nauseated about.

I had always been very hesitant about eating in the market place. It was the birthplace of many types of intestinal traumas. I had been lucky so far. Ian, on the other hand loved to eat in the market. No matter what town you were in throughout Latin America, there was always a market place.

Usually, at this time of the week, the market was a skeleton of what it was on Sunday. Today however, it was brimming with people, foods, wares to buy and many other strange and fascinating things. The townspeople were preparing for the holiday.

    We passed by the herb and spice area. There were all types of interesting items, such as many varieties of dried bugs. Yum, yum! There were also many types of cactus to eat. Yum, yum, yum! Ian stopped at a stand where a weary, middle-aged woman offered a taste of dried bugs. He tried to get me to eat the sample that the woman was holding out to me. I looked at him and gave him a "go ahead" nod of my head. He laughed and then took the dried grasshoppers and swallowed them. He gave the woman a few centavos and we were on our way. We needed to buy some food to take back to El Portal. We walked along other parts of the market and we were able to buy fresh cheese that was similar to goat cheese. We got eggs, tortillas, avocados, tomatoes, chilies and some different types of fruit. This was a lot to carry. I was in charge of the eggs, and Ian had the rest. I was standing with my back to Ian, looking at some interesting fruit, when he came up behind me, put his arms around my middle and kissed me on the neck. I was grateful that he was being demonstrative again.

    The rest of the afternoon was spent exploring the market and the other shops in the immediate vicinity. As we were walking around the town and through some of the little side streets, I could see signs, in Spanish, which said, "Card Reading, Aromatherapy and Crystals." There were obviously a few psychics and healers in town. I got the impression that there were a lot of spiritual people in the Tepoztlan area.

    As we meandered down a side street off the main square, we walked by a store that had tarot cards, pendulums and other metaphysical merchandise in the window. Ian and I were immediately attracted to the place. Ian of course, wanted to talk to the owner. He wanted to see if they were interested in his Mayan astrology conversion charts. He didn't have a prototype of what was to become the Mayan Calendar and

Conversion Codex at that point, but he did have his charts. The man in the store said that the owner, who was a woman, would be there tomorrow. He said that she was a scholar of the Mayan and Aztec calendars. What the sales person said really perked Ian up. There was a Mayan calendar scholar right in town! Ian wanted to come back to the store the next day.

When we left that store, Ian announced that he wanted to eat lunch in the marketplace. "Oh No!" I thought. I did not want to argue with him about where to eat. After all, he was beginning to be nice to me. I diligently followed him toward the food section. He sat down in front of a woman that was making tortillas on a small, flat metal pan that was placed on top of a large fifty-gallon metal drum. There were flames coming out of the metal drum. I sat down next to him and was ready for whatever. The woman rattled off the menu as soon as we sat down. I had a bowl of chicken soup and tortillas. Ian had Pazole, which is soup with tripe or cow intestines in it. YUMMM! I explained to Ian what was in Pazole. He laughed and wanted it anyway.

After we got done eating, we decided to head back to El Portal. I really enjoyed walking through the town. I admired the interesting way they decorated their houses and their yards. There would be a lot of attention-grabbing sights the following day for the holiday.

During the walk back to El Portal, Ian was in a good mood, which meant that he was talking non-stop. Pablo was also eager to have Ian make jewelry for him. He wanted to sell Ian's jewelry to the Mexicans from Mexico City that frequented El Portal. Pablo wanted Ian to come live at El Portal. Fortunately, Ian realized that would not be a good idea. Ian needed to be where he had access to Internet and an airport. Both of those things were far away from El Portal at that time.

We were almost to El Portal when it started to rain. I was feeling good, Ian was being nice, and all was right with the world. When we arrived, El Portal was filled with people who were starting to make dinner. We noticed that now there were a lot of people there. It was time for us all to come together. They were Mexicans who were visiting from Mexico City to enjoy the holiday. We had a great communal dinner that night. I was able to talk to a lot of the people, but Ian was at a loss. Most of them did not speak English. I noticed that Ian was smiling a lot at the beautiful women. They were all in couples. "See, there is a God!"

After dinner, we sat around a bonfire. Ian was not being his fabulously demonstrative self, but he was polite to me. We went back to the teepee together. He did not want to make love, but he did kiss me good night. Things were getting a wee bit better.

The next day was filled with excitement. I felt that even before I got out of the teepee. There was going to be a great fiesta in the plaza of Tepoztlan.

IAN, PABLO, BEATRICE AND I STARTED THE WALK TO town after breakfast. Once we arrived in town, I felt free to enjoy the celebration.

I loved to be in a Latin American town during a fiesta. The whole place felt so alive! Everyone was busy. There were all kinds of foods being made, and there were all kinds of belongings for sale. Ian said that we had time to walk around for a bit. There was going to be a ceremony in about a half hour. We spent the time looking at all the great merchandise stalls.

Next, we headed to the ceremonial area where the Independence Day celebration was about to take place. We were standing behind some young children that were pointing to their friends and relatives and giggling. Then a band started to play and lines of children dressed in school uniforms emerged. The presentation was very militaristic. They marched in formation and made several straight rows. Next they started to sing some Mexican songs.

I was glad to see that the educational system had improved since I had been in Mexico. When I had been there in the 1970's, I had seen the school system. Most children did not go to grammar school at all. The ones that were able to go, because their parents could afford it, had to sit on the dirt floor and practice writing on big pieces of brown paper. In many of the little schools I saw in towns like Tepoztlan, the children had very little opportunity to be educated. It was good to see that the children were getting a better education and that the school system had improved.

Tepoztlan had definitely prospered in the time that I had been away. I felt that was due in part to the tourism that came their way. Tepoztlan had a small pyramid on top of a mountain overlooking the city. I had seen a steady stream of people climbing up it when we had first arrived in town. I climbed up it myself when I had visited on my school vacations. Now Ian wanted to climb up to it. He was determined that he was going to do that the next day.

After the school children filed out, next came a message from the mayor of Tepoztlan. I really couldn't make out most of it. Next, we saw some Mexican folk dancers. They were wearing costumes that were the traditional clothing from this region. The large flower designs on their costumes were famous in this part of Mexico. I loved watching dancing. The dancers moved with grace and precision. Then they introduced a man who was going to give a long speech. When this man started to speak, we decided that we were going to wander around.

I was ready to have lunch. I let Ian do the picking again for our mid-day meal. He enjoyed looking at all the food stands. He looked at everything and finally selected a stand that had been set up just for the celebration. We sat down, and a bowl with pork in a thick soup with beans was handed to me. I sat down at the table and Ian started to laugh at me. He knew what I was thinking. He knew that I was completely appalled at the idea of eating this food. Being that I was on my best behavior, I leaned over, gave him a peck on the cheek and plunged into my lunch.

The rest of the day was really agreeable. After wandering around awhile we went back to El Portal and had a leisurely afternoon.

Pablo made another big bond fire at El Portal that night, in honor of the fiesta. That night, at El Portal, there was a lot of drinking, dancing, laughing and lovemaking.

The day after the fiesta, Ian and I went into town again. He had to climb the pyramid. After we got into Tepoztlan, I decided to wait in a cafe that Pablo said was the best in town. I enjoyed a lot of coffee and a hearty, leisurely breakfast while Ian walked up the steps that led to the little pyramid.

It took Ian two hours to make it back to the café. He looked triumphant, but worn out when he staggered into the café and plopped down in the seat next to me. After he rested a bit, he wanted to go to the shop with the tarot cards. In our haste to get back to the tepees the day before, we had forgotten to stop at that store. When we arrived there, the owner was not to be found. Ian was disappointed, but I felt we would meet her when the time was right.

We had a sweet farewell with Pablo and Beatrice the next morning. We returned to Mexico City on the Mercedes bus and had one more night in another glamorous hotel in Mexico City. All of our flights and connections went smoothly on our return to the U. S. A.

WHEN WE GOT BACK TO PHOENIX AND MY LITTLE apartment, I needed to decompress from the exploit that I had just experienced. After a few days, I was able to merge back into my existence in Cave Creek. My massage clients where whining. That was fortunate because I needed to catch up financially. Ian seemed to be getting over my shortcomings as an accountant and we were getting back to our natural state of affection and flow.

With the blessing of Don Alejandro, Ian felt renewed about his work. He wanted to focus upon manifesting the Mayan Calendar and Conversion Codex. He had the name and idea clearly in his mind. He felt that now it was time to birth the product that would bring his charts to the world.

He shared everything that was in his mind with me. He always asked me for my opinion of whatever he wanted to do. He seemed to have great respect for my perspective, but did not always accept everything I said. I was just happy that he asked for my input. When he was going to use something that I had suggested, he made a point of telling me that he was glad that I had contributed.

The Mayan Calendar and Conversion Codex were coming together nicely. The project needed money that neither of us had. In order to get his show on the road, Ian started making model cars for a man that lived on the East Coast. I supported us while Ian spent the money he made on bringing his projects to life. I was glad to be able to help, but my income was not really adequate to support two people. Yet, somehow, I was able to provide what was needed. Ian had told me a zillion times that he wanted me to benefit from all of his projects. The anticipation of being prosperous motivated us. We both had high hopes for the future. It was a very busy and exciting time.

Ian started contacting the other Mayan calendar scholars that he admired to tell them about his experience with Don Alejandro. There were a lot of emails and phone calls coming in from people like John Major Jenkins, Bruce Scofield and Kenneth Johnson. These men were considered prominent authorities on the Mayan calendar and Mayan astrology. They all agreed with Ian that the count of the Tzolkin used by the Maya in the Guatemalan highlands was the accurate count for this sacred calendar of the Maya. Ian told me that these men were impressed with his charts. Every now and then I answered the phone and was honored to have a chat with them.

We toiled over the pictures, the background and layouts for the Mayan Calendar and Conversion Codex until we were pleased with them. My kitchen table became the layout board. We found a large mural that we faded out and used as a background for the charts and other information. We had an empty space and Ian filled it with a picture I liked. We made several mock ups of the codex using my bottom-of-the-line computer and printer. The names of the day lords used by Jose Arguelles were changed to those Ian had received from

Alex. The descriptions of the day lords and numbers were made simple and concise. When the Mayan Calendar and Conversion Codex had been assembled, we felt we had created a product that was a pure representation of the knowledge Ian had received.

By the end of 1998, the Mayan Calendar and Conversion Codex were born. We made a small batch of 1000. Ian had them laminated to make sure that they would last a long time. After the codex was birthed, Ian went to many of the New Age shops in Phoenix and Sedona and found it fairly easy to sell them.

The fact that Ian valued my participation in all his projects made me feel very special. It was great to be involved in something so innovative and stimulating. By working on the project with him, I stabilized my knowledge about Mayan astrology. I now felt comfortable talking to people about the astrology. I did not have the flamboyance that Ian always displayed when he talked about Mayan astrology, but I did feel confident sharing the knowledge I had gleaned by being part of his life.

THE FIRST PUBLIC PRESENTATION OF THE MAYAN Calendar and Conversion Codex took place when it was printed in a magazine called Magical Blend, in the beginning of 1999. There were many typos that aggravated Ian, but he was happy that the Mayan Calendar and Conversion Codex had been published in an internationally renowned magazine.

In March of 1999, Ian found out about a Crystal Skull convention that was to be held in Sedona, AZ. This was an hour and a half drive from our place in Cave Creek. It was being headed by a crop circle researcher named Chet Snow. Ian had always been friendly with Chet Snow. Chet was willing to give Ian the opportunity to do a lecture on Mayan astrology. It was to be his first public lecture on Mayan astrology and his system of finding the Mayan astrology sign with his conversion charts. He was eager to have my help with this venture. Ian respected the fact that I was a good teacher and lecturer. Together we created a format for the lecture. I was delighted to be in the center of his new focus. He was spending most of his time with his jewelry. This gave him great joy but did not give us anything to harmonize about. The lecture gave us something new to work on together.

He spent many days going over his notes and talking to me about the event. He wanted to have a slide presentation. He went on a quest to procure a slide projector. Then he took his drawings of the day lords and had slides made of them. He was excited about the idea of being in front of people and talking to them about Mayan astrology. This would be the beginning of a career in lecturing that would go on after Ian and I had parted ways.

A couple weeks before the May event, Ian told me that we would be seeing Hortencia and the man that we had met at Don Alejandro's house when we went to Guatemala City. I would be able to be at the convention as much as I wanted because Ian had a booth there and was also a lecturer. I always liked going to expos. It would be nice to be behind the scenes in this one.

The weekend of the expo came quickly. Ian was really taking charge. I was very proud of him. He had found a place for us to stay in Sedona with a strange psychic that he had met during his travels. We went to the hotel where the conference was being held and set up on Friday night. I went back to Cave Creek that night because I had to work on Saturday.

When I returned to Sedona and the convention on Saturday evening, Ian looked despondent. He had sold very little jewelry. He was a bit nervous about his lecture. He was scheduled to be the last lecturer on Sunday. I reassured him that all was going to be fine. I caught a glimpse of Hortencia while I was talking to Ian. I was pleased to see her. She was selling jewelry and other Mayan trinkets. She was there with the bodyguard/interpreter that had been at Don Alejandro's house in Guatemala City. I decided to go over and say hello. I still wanted to connect with her and be a part of the indigenous events that she sponsored in Santa Fe. She was polite, but reserved with me. I left her booth with the impression that she did not want to be involved with me. As things turned out, she was not open to anyone that was there.

Ian told me that there was going to be a Mayan Fire Ceremony at dawn on Sunday morning, led by Hortencia and the man I will call the bodyguard. I wanted to see if it was the same ceremony that I had learned with Claudia and Alex in Santa Fe.

That night I did not sleep very well. I didn't like to get up at dawn, but I did not want to miss the ceremony. When Ian and I got to the hotel the next morning, the ceremony was about to begin. Before the ceremony started, all the participants were all asked to stand in a line. There were about twenty of us. We were each given a little round piece of Copal to throw into the fire. The plate piled high with sage looked the same as the one that we saw Claudia make.

Ian was standing behind me as we waited in line to put our prayers and our wishes into the fire along with the Copal. While I was standing in line, I started crying. I don't know why exactly. I thought that it was from all the stress of the weekend and not sleeping well. I was crying softly all the time that I was waiting in line. It took about 15 minutes to get to the front. I was next in line to throw my Copal in the fire, when the bodyguard came up to me. He leaned over and whispered in my ear, "Don't worry. It will all be over soon."

I didn't know what he meant, but I just nodded in thanks for the message. Then it was my turn and I threw my Copal into the fire. I asked for happiness, peace and prosperity. Hortencia looked at me as I threw my Copal into the fire, but did not smile or make any gesture. After Ian had thrown his into the fire, we went to breakfast. I just had coffee.

I began to feel better as the day went on. I enjoyed sitting at Ian's booth and talking to people about his jewelry. Ian gave his lecture in the early afternoon. When it was time for him to start, he got up on the stage and started fiddling with his borrowed slide projector. I passed out the handouts for his lecture. I felt uplifted as I gave Ian's paperwork to the small group of curious attendees. As he began his presentation, I sat down to listen to his maiden voyage into the realm of lecturing. I was impressed at his presentation. He spoke in a slow, deliberate, easy to follow manner. He did a great job.

    Shortly after Ian's lecture was over, Chet made an announcement. He said that all the crystal skulls were going to come up on stage. We would all have a chance to walk by them and feel their energy. We had to leave the main room for a while. Only the skulls and their owners were allowed to be inside while the skulls were being arranged on the stage. When we came back to the conference room, in about a half hour, all the crystal skulls, big and small, ancient and new, were lined up on the stage. A line formed on the right side of the stage. I found myself in the middle of this line that moved slowly. When it was my turn to go up on stage I felt excited yet reverent. I slowly passed all the skulls and took a moment to run my hand above the top of each one. I took a longer moment with the ones that I felt were the most powerful for me. I definitely felt the energy coming from a big white skull named Max. Some of the smaller skulls were also powerful.

    After we had all viewed the skulls and been able to experience their energy, Chet got up on stage and said that Hortencia was going to read a letter from Don Alejandro. "How inspiring!" I thought. It would be good to hear from him. Without a smile, Hortencia walked up on the stage and began to read the letter. In a very formal manner, she stated that Don Alejandro and the Mayan Council of Elders that he represented did not want anyone talking about, teaching or spreading knowledge of the Mayan calendar or Mayan astrology. They did not want people who were not of Mayan decent sharing the sacred knowledge with people who were not Mayan. In the same letter, it was also stated that the crystal skulls that had been taken from the Maya, and the whole area of Central Mexico, needed to be returned to their people. The letter specifically named the Mitchell Hedges skull. The letter demanded that it be returned to the Maya.

    For those of you who are not up on all the crystal skull information, the Mitchell Hedges skull was the first skull that was taken out of Central America. It was found by an explorer named Mitchell Hedges. This skull is unique beyond any other skull that has ever been found. It has a jaw that moves. It has been examined thoroughly and scientists have come to the conclusion that the Mitchell Hedges skull was not made by human hands or human machinery. Suffice to say that this skull is potent. Many other skulls have been found since the Mitchell Hedges skull was discovered. They have been sold to non-Mayans by starving Hispanics who pillaged the ruins or dug them up while planting crops. None of the many skulls that now travel the world on display have the mystique or the energy of the Mitchell Hedges skull. Even the most notable skull that was at the conference, Max, was very crudely made compared to the Mitchell Hedges skull.

When Hortencia came off the stage, there was dead silence. Obviously, Chet Snow had no idea what the letter contained. Everyone was a bit stunned. Ian was speechless. We all filed out of the workshop with our jaws dragging down to our chests. This information must have been devastating to Ian, more than he ever let on. He must have felt betrayed by Don Alejandro. He had gone through so much to get his approval. Now he was being rejected by him! Ian didn't say much for the rest of the day. We packed up and went home in silence.

IN JUNE, AN E-MAIL CAME TO US THAT TALKED ABOUT the upcoming eclipse that would be in August of 1999. The e-mail said that it would be very important to be in the spot that you felt was right for you. The energy of the eclipse would activate your true essence. The e-mail went on to say that you should be in your selected place a few days before the eclipse. You had to be in the same area for a few days after the eclipse as well. After the eclipse, you needed to stay in a 150-mile radius of the exact location you would be in for the eclipse. Following these instructions would assist you to focus the full impact of the eclipse to manifest what you desired in your life. The eclipse would imprint you with the future you choose to manifest.

Of course Ian decided that he wanted to go to Mexico. I wanted to be by Ian's side for this event. I decided that I would go with him to Mexico in August. We were determined to spend the time at El Portal. We were also going to spend some time at the ruins of Teotihuacán. These ruins are right outside of Mexico City. They are within the 150mile radius. Teotihuacán was an Aztec ceremonial center. This site was home to many ancient tribes in Mesoamerica before the Aztecs took it over. It had also been the site of mass executions where the beating hearts of the sacrifices were held up to the cheering crowds.

This trip was not going to have as much traveling as the last one. We were going to arrive in Acapulco and spend two nights there and enjoy the beach. Next we would go to Taxco and pass the night there. Taxco is the silver jewelry capitol of Mexico and very close to Mexico City. Then we would travel through Mexico City to Amatlan, where we would spend the rest of the time. We would be at El Portal when the eclipse took place.

At the same time, there was also a lot of information going around in e-mails about the Y2K scare. These e-mails put Ian into a fear mode. He felt that he would be safe in Mexico when all the computers crashed and chaos prevailed.

As we were getting ready to go to Mexico in August, I was looking forward to the trip. Traveling brought out the romance in us.

FINALLY THE DAY CAME WHEN WE WERE TO GET ON THE plane and go back to the land of the Maya. My experience of landing in Acapulco was similar to my last trip. I felt slammed up against a mountain of heat and humidity as soon as I got out of the airplane. Even though it was about 8 p. m. in Acapulco, the heat made the humid air hard to breathe.

We got to the taxi area quickly. Ian took charge and was able to procure us two spaces in a modern looking van. This van took us on a scenic tour of the town that night. There were several young, gorgeous women in the van with us. As we drove through the hills surrounding Acapulco, we saw some of the splendor of the wealthy. The driver started dropping off these young women in front of mansions that overlooked the bay. Ian was very impressed not only with the palaces that overlooked the town, but with the fact that these women had no luggage. They just walked up to the front door of these palaces and the doors opened for them.

In due course, we were the only passengers left in the van. It was getting on toward 11 p. m. We had not reserved a hotel ahead of time, so Ian asked the driver to show us a good one. That turned out to be a big mistake! The driver took us for a ride in many ways. It must have been taxi driver karma, coming back to us for what we put the taxi driver through when we went to El Portal. He stopped in front of a hotel that had a mermaid at the entrance. The taxi driver and Ian went into the lobby. Ian came out and told me that he had paid for two nights, which was the minimum.

I was too hot and sweaty to complain. We were escorted to a room that was next to a swimming pool. The water in the pool looked black. When we got to the room, the front desk clerk/bellman showed us the large fan on a stand, which was our only source of cool air during our stay. Having spent many years in the desert, I understood cooling. I put a wet towel over the fan, and it started to blow cool air on us. I was exhausted, so I was able to fall asleep easily, even in the small, sweltering room.

I awoke the next day to find that our Acapulco nightmare was in full bloom. We heard people splashing in the pool. I opened the curtains and saw children and adults diving into a pool that was full of dark grey water. Yes, we were in Acapulco and had been victims of the "Taxi Driver Rip Off." He obviously got a kick back for bringing fresh victims to the mermaid.

I did try to make the best of it that day. We played at the beach. Ian enjoyed watching all the fine-looking women in their bathing suits cavort in the waves. We had lunch at a charming seaside restaurant on the main thoroughfare. As evening approached, I told Ian I did not want to go back to the hotel. We wandered around until dark and then had dinner at a restaurant that was right on the sand. It specialized in fresh fish and big margaritas. We both got a little crazy at dinner and got into drinking. We were singing our favorite Karaoke songs as we walked back to the hotel. I wanted to be anesthetized. That way the hotel situation would not bother me. I collapsed on the bed, in front of the fan with the towel on it, and passed the night in a dark void, devoid of dreams.

When I awoke, I felt pretty good considering all the alcohol I had consumed. The goddess of the Agave cactus had smiled upon me, and I was able to function quite well. We got dressed and out of the hotel quickly.

ANOTHER TAXI TOOK US TO THE BUS STATION. WE WERE bound for Taxco. We arrived at this superb center of jewelry making by the early afternoon. We found a simple, quaint motel near the bus station and settled in. It was a short walk into the main area of Taxco. We were both ravenous and quickly found a quaint rooftop restaurant to stop our stomachs from growling. It gave us a great vantage point to look out over the town. As we ate lunch, we could see the whole city of whitewashed buildings with their crimson tile roofs. Taxco was built on several hillsides. I was fascinated with the cobblestone streets and the way the homes and shops seemed to cascade down the side of the mountains.

This town was immaculate and well preserved. There were many churches for a town this size. I realized that the town was so well preserved because it was a very popular tourist stop. It was also a place where many wealthy Mexicans came to shop as well.

We spent the rest of that day and as much as we could of the next going to every jewelry shop in the town. Ian was in an idyllic state the whole time we were there. He knew what it took to make all the beautiful pieces of jewelry we were seeing. Most of the shop owners spoke English, so he was able to express himself freely. He had some of his pieces with him. The jewelers of Taxco were impressed with his work. Some even wanted to buy his pieces. Ian knew that they could copy them easily, so he always declined. The experience was good for Ian. The interest in his work gave him a much needed boost.

In the early evening, we arrived in Mexico City and settled into a nice hotel. We had arranged to stay in a hotel that was in the upscale part of town called the Zona Rosa. Our room was modern and had all the amenities of a four star hotel. That night we found a Karaoke bar around the corner and went to have some amusement. I thought it interesting that the majority of Mexican people sang songs in English. Ian performed his favorite from the Eurhythmics: Missionary Man. He drove the audience wild. Everyone was cheering and clapping as he walked back to our table and gave me a hug.

The next day, we were on the bus by mid-morning and in Cuernavaca by the afternoon. I had now had enough of taxi drivers. I told the one we chose, in Spanish, to just take us to the plaza in Tepoztlan. From the plaza, we took a van that is called a Pesero, out to Amatlan. The van stays at the plaza and loads up with farmers and country folk about every 15 minutes. For what used to be a Peso, but now was more like five Pesos, you could get a ride all the way out to the plaza at Amatlan. We were able to do the short walk to El Portal easily.

Pablo was not there when we hopped over the wall of the kitchen, but we did not need his help. It felt good to be back there. The place was deserted. We just waited, drank the coffee that had been left in the kitchen, and let out deep sights of relief. We were at our destination at last. The sky was full of heavy clouds that soon dropped their sweet, cool moisture on El Portal.

WHEN WE RETURNED TO EL PORTAL, WE FOUND THAT the circumstances had changed a bit. Beatrice was gone, and her replacement was called Inez. She was also young, in her early twenties. She was also very striking. One quality that I found interesting about Inez was that she was also very spiritual.

Inez was petite with long, straight, black hair, latte-colored skin, and dark, almond shaped eyes. She had a waiflike quality that reminded one of Audrey Hepburn. She ate no food during the day. She just drank juice. She also wandered around the property a lot. The story that she told, in very good English, was that she had come to El Portal with a boyfriend. She was like many of the young seekers that we had seen the first time we were there. She had an experience when she was at El Portal, which she feels bonded her to the property. She came to El Portal to live soon after. She came to be with the earth and the property.

On our first morning at El Portal, Inez was wandering the grounds. As we had breakfast, we could see her talking to the land and singing to it. She was touching the rocks and having a great communion with the earth. In between drinking juice and cooing over Pablo, this was how she spent her day.

After resting that whole day, we made plans with Inez and Pablo to go to Teotihuacán the following day. Pablo seemed to have this excursion organized. No more taxi drivers! We would drive through Mexico City and spend the night at a hotel near the sight, so we could get an early start and have the whole day to roam the ruins.

After a hair-raising drive through Mexico City the next day, we arrived at a little motel near Teotihuacán.

We got to the ruins early in the morning. For the occasion, Ian had brought some "magic mushrooms." We ate them just before we went into the site. We flowed into the compound with several hundred other tourists as the mushrooms started to take effect.

The Teotihuacán site is made up of several pyramids joined by a long processional walkway. The first pyramid we scaled was the Pyramid of the Sun. This is the largest structure in the complex. When we got to the top, we found the panoramic scene before us to be extraordinary. We could see at least fifty miles in every direction. The surrounding land was flat and green, with few trees and sparse shrubbery.

We decided to do a ceremony at each one of the pyramids as the mushrooms brought us closer to the gods of the Maya. Each one of us was a day lord of a different direction. I was white for the north, Ian was yellow for the south, Pablo was red for the east, and Inez was blue for the west.

The view from on top of the Pyramid of the Sun was spectacular. The whole sprawling ceremonial center was before us. With many people looking on, we took our positions and began the ceremony. We let Ian lead the ceremony since he was the most verbal of the group. We stood in place and listened to Ian. Ceremony brought out his zeal for communicating with the ancestors. When he was done, we all raised our hands to the sky and did our personal prayers of thanks. We all sent our prayers to the gods simultaneously. Then we were done and ready to go on to the next pyramid.

Ian standing on the Pyramid of the Sun at Teotihuacán.

The next structure that we went to was the Pyramid of the Moon. It was to the right of the Pyramid of the Sun at the far north end of the complex. That was the creepiest place for me. At the base of the Pyramid of The Moon is a circular structure that looked like it was constructed for people to lie on as they were sacrificed. It looked like a large daisy, with rectangular petals jutting out from the center. These petals were just wide enough for a person to lie down on. It was easy to imagine the priest standing at the top of the pyramid looking down at the victims below. Ian had told me that the sacrificial victims were given heavy doses of hallucinogens, probably mushrooms, before they came out in front of the crowds waiting to witness their deaths. There was no resistance from the victims. They were in a state of rapture and did not feel the pain that their sacrifice inflicted upon their body.

When we got to the top of the Pyramid of the Moon, we were in awe of the magnificence of the day. Pablo was the only one of the four of us who had been to these ruins before. He enjoyed our enthusiasm. We did our ceremony there too. Most people did not appear to care. Many people stood around to watch us. We stayed up there for a long time. Ian took a picture of Pablo with his hand out and a butterfly perched upon it.

We made our way down to the ground, and we were on to the next structure. When I first arrived at the Teotihuacán complex, I was aghast to see that the original stonework had been covered over by cement. I did realize that there were so many people coming to this site, that the stones needed to be covered up to keep them from disintegrating.

We spent the entire day at the ruins. Pablo brought some water for us, which was a good thing. I realized that my arms were burning from exposure to the sun. There were no rain clouds to buffer the intense sunlight that was beating down upon us. The power of the mushrooms helped me to ignore what was happening to my body and to enjoy the day.

It was late afternoon when we reached the final pyramid. This is the pyramid with all of the serpent heads of Quetzalcoatl. The steps to the pyramid were blocked off, so no one could walk up them. The heads of the Plumed Serpents were perfectly preserved. They were remarkable in their detail. There must have been twenty uniquely carved serpent heads that lined the stairs that led to the pyramid's apex. I was able to touch the original stones at this pyramid, even though we were not able to walk on them. The stones felt soothing. It is what I had been waiting for the whole day. This place felt very sacred and pure. I wanted to stay there for a long time, but my group was moving me on. We were still feeling the euphoria of the mushrooms as Pablo drove us back to the peace and verdant splendor of Amatlan that evening. This was the end of our journey through Teotihuacán. To this day, I feel that the ceremony we did there was important in some way. All ceremony done with pure intentions helps our planet.

BY THE TIME WE ARRIVED AT THE TEPEES, THE PAIN FROM my sunburn was in high gear. Pablo put some homemade ointment on my shoulders and my arms. That did help take the sting away. I still slept well that night, even though my body was burning.

The next day was the day of the eclipse. There was going to be a big ceremony that night at El Portal, as well as a sweat lodge. Before we went to Teotihuacán, Pablo had been insistent that I experience the sweat lodge. When the night came however, he could see that my sunburn would be too painful for me to be inside with the immense heat that was generated during a sweat lodge ceremony. I was thankful that I was able to stay outside the lodge and experience its energy while the ceremony was going on inside.

As evening came, El Portal was filled with young seekers who were coming to this sacred land to experience the energy of the eclipse. Only a few of them were going to participate in the sweat lodge ceremony. The stones for the sweat lodge had been heating up in a nearby fire pit for several hours. Just before the sweat lodge ceremony was to begin, the attendees formed a line outside the small, oval shaped, wooden frame that had been covered with many blankets. I was to stay outside, along with a man who was helping Pablo. The young man was to transport the glowing, scarlet rocks with a shovel, into a pit that was in the center of the lodge.

Before anyone entered the sweat lodge, Pablo used a feather fan to spread sage smoke throughout the aura of each person. This was done to purify their energy fields before they were to participate in the Native American ritual. After ten people had squeezed into the lodge, that would have been comfortable seating for six people, Ian and Pablo entered last. A heavy blanket was then pulled down over the entrance of the lodge. All the participants were sitting in the dark. From my experience inside sweat lodges, I knew that everyone inside was engulfed in total darkness. I remembered not even being able to see the person sitting next to me. Everyone inside had now symbolically entered the womb of the Earth Mother.

When the sweat lodge ceremony got underway, Pablo started to sing songs and drum. Then he opened the flap covering the entrance, and the first of the red-hot stones to be used that night were taken into the sweat lodge. After the stones had been brought in, the flap over the entrance was closed. I could hear the sound of water being poured on the stones. The stone people, as the rocks are called, made hissing sounds. The stones were singing and imparting their wisdom to those inside. I could feel the energy of the sweat lodge ceremony building, even being on the outside.

In most sweat lodge ceremonies, it is customary to bring the stones in four times. Each time the stones are brought in, a new intention is created by the group. Everyone offers their prayers out loud to the Earth Mother and the grandmother and grandfather spirits that are in attendance.

I could hear Ian's voice as he sang the songs with the group and spoke his truth. I was having a powerful experience during the sweat lodge ceremony. Even though I was sitting outside; it was easy for me to merge with the energy that was being generated inside. I felt that I had entered an altered state where I could commune with the ancient ones as well. I offered my prayers during each round along with the others inside. At the end of the sweat lodge, all the people came out looking flushed and radiant.

After the sweat lodge, the night of the eclipse turned into an all-night vigil. Ian and I stayed up talking with the other attendees. They were mostly young, inspired and excited to be out of Mexico City and in Nature. They really appreciated being in a place that was green and bursting with life. We all went to the kitchen, where a feast of fruit, cheese, and yogurt was waiting. When you have been very dehydrated, your body appreciates melons and other fruit.

At one o'clock in the morning the eclipse took place in Mexico. Inez decided to blow a conch shell to welcome the eclipse. She started walking around the compound singing and blowing the conch shell. We all thought it was great at first. We all took turns trying to blow the shell, but Inez had that skill mastered. She walked around the property all night blowing the conch shell. Pablo gave her a stern lecture and made her blow it softly, right as we all went to bed. As I was falling off to sleep that night, I could still hear that shell being blown in the distance. It was going on when I woke up too. The frail little thing had stayed up all night blowing the shell and wandering around the property. She went to bed, up in the tree house, as the rest of us were getting up.

We had a great time getting to know everyone that morning. We met a woman named Marisa from the northern part of Mexico. She was a large woman who spoke English very well. She was also on vacation and staying at El Portal. I found her to be a great companion during our stay there.

AFTER THE CROWDS LEFT, IAN SET OUT TO ACCOMPLISH the task that he had assigned himself for the trip: to finish revising The Mayan Calendar and Conversion Codex. Ian and I had been in the middle of revising the codex before we came on this trip. He wanted to add more description for the day lords and the numbers. We planned to make the new codex larger. Ian adored writing, and wanted the next codex to have more verbiage than the original version. Ian waited to finish the rewrites in Mexico so he could get Pablo's input about the material.

The dining area of El Portal became Ian's study and writing room. That morning, Marisa and I took a walk around Amatlan. We returned to find Pablo and Ian discussing parts of the codex in the dining area. Pablo was encouraging Ian to change the names of the day lords. He thought that they needed to be easier to understand. That is how many of the day lord names came to be changed in the second codex. Ian's day lord, Ancestors, was later changed to Sun. My day lord name was eventually changed from Blade to Flint. The knife that was represented by Blade was often made out of flint.

    The next day, when I woke up, I started to get dressed in the tepee. Ian had already gone to the dining area for the morning. I started to put on some loose cotton pants that had been hanging on a rope that went all the way around the inside of the tepee. Much to my surprise, my pants had become home to a tiny, yet highly venomous insect. This creature was small but carried a mighty sting. As I was putting on my pants, it stung me on the back of the knee. I let out a scream that had the whole complex running to my tepee!

    That was the beginning of the most painful experience that I have ever had. What I experienced that day must have been invented by a demon from the underworld. All I could do for the first half hour was cry. I whimpered constantly as I felt the top of my calf and the bottom of my thigh start to grow numb and cold. The venom was spreading from my knee up and down my leg. This bug had figured out the supreme method to inflict torment. The poison seemed as if it was time released. The pain would subside, only to start up again in 15 minutes. After about an hour and a half of this, I took Ian aside and told him that the bite was serious. I felt that I needed help. Finally, Ian spoke to Pablo about the bite. In a few minutes, Pablo came back and gave me an anti-venom pill that did stop the cold from spreading up and down my leg. Unfortunately, the pill did nothing to lessen the pain.

    After I had been attended to, Ian and Pablo went back to their task of examining and rewriting the original Mayan Calendar and Conversion Codex. After another hour of suffering passed, I started to have an experience that I can only describe as going into an altered state from the venom. I started to feel like I was sitting in a fish bowl looking out. I was listening to Ian and Pablo, but they seemed muffled and blurry to me. I felt that I was being separated from everyone else. The venom took me to another state of consciousness. I didn't have hallucinations. I didn't see any patterns or colors like I had with the Ayawaska, but the venom put me in a strange, in-between-the-worlds-type of awareness. I wish this altered state of mind had taken away the torture, but that was still there. It was obvious, from my experience, that some of the venom had gotten to my brain. I can only imagine what I would have felt like if I had not taken the anti-venom pill!

While I was in an altered state of mind, I was being shown that someone was going to take my place. I could not turn away or ignore what I was seeing. The venom was making me sit still and witness the union of Ian and Pablo.

I felt I was also being shown that my time with Ian was coming to an end. The venom was showing me. I was sitting right next to Ian, and it was as if I was not there. He was putting his energy into another person. That was meant to happen. I had to accept that he needed to make his life with others. The venom was presenting me with a vivid illustration that my life with Ian would soon transform.

Other people, like Pablo, were going to take over my role. Okay, I get it. Could the pain stop now, please? The demon did not listen. He kept pumping misery into my body.

The time released, on and off again condition of the venom was really traumatizing me. By bedtime, the agony had only diminished slightly. I lay in bed awake, while Ian was on the other side of the tepee, sleeping soundly. As I would start to drift into the sleep state, another cycle of the pain would begin and wake me up. This happened three times while I was trying to sleep that night. Finally, I was so exhausted from the whole situation that I passed out. I went into a deep sleep. This happened about 10 p. m. At that point, I had been suffering for 12 hours.

A couple of hours later I woke up, and all the agony was gone. I got the impression that I was having a dream that I was pain free, and went back to sleep. When I actually did wake up about 7 a. m. the next morning, the pain was really gone! I got up, walked around and saw that the torture was indeed over.

I knew that it was not my body alone that had been able to process all the venom in such a short time, even with an anti-venom pill. I sensed that something else had happened. I did not know why the pain had vanished, but I felt that a miracle had happened. I had no pain at all, no swelling, no numbness, nothing to remind me of the nightmare I had lived through the day before. The only way I knew that something had happened at all, was that I had a little red mark on the back of my knee, where the insect had punctured my skin.

Pablo thought it was remarkable that I had recovered so quickly. I guess he knew something about the bug that had taken over my life the previous day. Yet, he said he knew very little about the bug. Instead, he suggested that Marisa and I go talk to a shaman who lived in Amatlan. That day we did not go to see him. I was too tired to make the trip. I just wanted to rest and relax. I was thankful for the freedom from the ordeal I had been through the day before.

THE FOLLOWING MORNING, MARISA AND I SET OUT walking to the place where the shaman lived. We left Ian and Pablo working on the codex in the kitchen. We walked by some rivers and then up a small hill to a little shack on the top of the hill. Marisa knocked on the door of the shack. A very grungy, forty something man emerged. He looked like he had not bathed in a long time, yet there were no offensive odors. The only pieces of furniture in his little wood shack were a bed, a table and two chairs. There were some herbs hanging upside down from the ceiling and some packaged food on shelves along the wall. My mind went to the practical, and I thought about the fact that there was no outhouse anywhere around. He was definitely in tune with nature.

Marisa and I went inside his little home and sat down on the chairs he offered us. He sat on his bed. She knew, but I really didn't at the time, that it was an honor for us to be there. His invitation into his home was a sign that he was willing to listen to my story. Marisa seemed to be impressed with the man. She took a very humble stance with him. She spoke to him in Spanish with a respectful tone in her voice. The shaman's name was Gilberto. He was tall and slender, with long, stringy brown hair that was pulled back in a ponytail. I was able to take the position of an observer, like I had on the day Ian and I met with Don Alejandro.

Marisa was a very formal woman. She approached the man with all the formality and respect that the President of Mexico would have received. I understood most of what she was saying and felt that she was doing a good job of speaking for me. Marisa took the roundabout course that one must take with a man of power. She did not to ask him directly about the bite I had received. She made a lot of small talk and gave Gilberto the opportunity to offer the information we were seeking. Marisa and the medicine man chatted for about 15 minutes before the issue at hand was addressed.

After Marisa described in detail my agony, Gilberto asked to look at my leg. I rolled up my pants and showed him the little red mark, which was all that was left of that horrible day. He looked at the puncture wound and then looked at me. He was silent for a long moment. What Gilberto finally came around to saying, was that the bug that had stung me was very common in the area. He never mentioned the name of the bug. He went on to say that the pain of the sting, which I had described with Marisa's help, lasted for about two days. Many people had died from the sting of that bug. The toxins had been known to send a person into a trance or sometimes a coma. It took a long time to get the venom out of the body. People were often feeling the residue of the venom for days and weeks afterward.

The medicine man became very curious about me after he had heard my story. He said that he felt that I had been given some special assistance from the spirits to overcome the effects of the bite so quickly. I was not surprised, but I was impressed. The two talked for a bit more, and then we took our leave.

Many months later, after I moved to Sedona, I realized the connection between my totem animal, the jaguar, and this experience. I was taken on a shamanic journey by a woman who was an expert in totem animals. We were both surprised how strongly the jaguar came through during the journey. She told me that the jaguar often comes to people they work with in the dream state. The jaguar does much of its work in the dream state. I then remembered that the jaguar had first made itself known to me in the dreams I had at Claudia's house in Santa Fe. I now feel that the jaguar healed me that night in the tepee. Since the understanding of my totem animal has become clear to me, I feel secure that the jaguar is an ally that will always be by my side to protect and heal me in times of dire need.

AS MARISA AND I WALKED BACK TO EL PORTAL, I KNEW that I was blessed to have recovered so quickly. The information the medicine man conveyed verified that. After we got back, Marisa gave a blow by blow description to Pablo of what the shaman had said. Pablo was also silent for a long time. Then he stated that he, Ian and I were walking to town.

Ian was working at being nice to me. Pablo could see that I had no trouble keeping up with him and Ian. When the three of us arrived at the edge of Tepoztlan, Ian and I parted ways with Pablo. Ian took my hand and walked with me into the plaza. While we were strolling around the town, we found ourselves walking by the shop that we had stopped at last year. We walked in and saw the same tarot cards and other metaphysical trinkets that had been in the window the year before.

This time, the owner was there. She was a tall, slender, blond woman named Lila. She was younger than us. She was very amiable and spoke perfect English. This gave Ian the opportunity to rattle on about his conversion codex. She seemed to be very interested in what he was saying. Lila told us that she had spent her life studying the Mayan and Aztec calendars. She invited us to come over to her house the next day. She wrote down her address. We were both excited to talk to a Mayan calendar scholar from Mexico.

The next day, we got to town about an hour before the time of our appointment. We decided to take a taxi to her house. Pablo did not know where her house was. She did not give us detailed instructions, just the address. We thought that it would be better to get someone who knew the streets better than us. We went on a half hour taxi ride that should have only taken ten minutes. The taxi driver did not know exactly where the house was. But he finally found the address, with the help of many on lookers and a great deal of head bobbing and pointing. He dropped us off in front of a large gate. Once we went through the gate, we could see that we were standing in front of a large country manor. The grounds and the house overwhelmed us with their splendor. There was a short road, about 300 feet, which went through the middle of a well-manicured lawn and led to the house. As we were walking up to the house, we could see the large walled garden with abundant foliage and flowers. The house was three stories. It had a viewing deck on the top floor. It must have been a great place to watch the sunset. It had a large downstairs patio. While we sat there waiting, Lila came out to greet us. I was taken aback by the size of the place, but I did not want to feel intimidated. Houses like this are common in Mexico.

Lila took us up to her study. It was filled with many old Aztec drawings that were painted on tree bark. She had a lot of books spread about, but the room was fairly neat. She was very interested in Ian's charts. He had brought one to give her. We talked for a bit. Or should I say that she and Ian talked, while I listened. Lila told Ian that she wanted to examine his charts and that she would see us the day after tomorrow. That was fine; we were planning to be there for four more days.

We left the hacienda and walked to town to have some lunch. Town was very close. As we entered the plaza, I started to cringe inside at the thought of eating in the marketplace again. This time, Ian was feeling so good that we actually got to eat lunch in the real restaurant! After lunch, we poked around the market a bit, and then headed for El Portal.

Ian was excited about his connection with Lila. Ian talked to Pablo about our visit when we got home. Pablo thought that the connection was extremely positive.

WHEN WE CAME TO HER HOUSE THE SECOND TIME, LILA had some drinks and lunch waiting for us. She was a very gracious hostess. After a delicious meal, we went up to Lila's study and again, I was fascinated by her collection of pictures and books. I went over to look at the ones that attracted me.

She asked us to sit down and gestured to some couches in her study. After we were seated, she began by saying that she thought Ian's charts were very good. She stated that she worked with the Aztec calendar as well as the Mayan calendar and had studied them both extensively. She said that it was a well-accepted theory that the Mayan calendar actually came from the earlier Aztec calendar. They had the same day lords, but with different names. The Aztecs had the concepts of the numbers for 1-13 as well. Ian bantered back that the Aztecs may have had the concept of the calendar before the Mayans, but there were other aspects of the calendar that were purely Mayan. The Maya had definitely put their brand on the calendar.

Then Lila asked Ian a question. She asked him why his charts only went up to the year 2013. He laughed and then said that she must know that the Long Count calendar ends on 12/21/2012. He said that was the date that the world as we know it was going to end. He then started into his doomsday scenario. While he was going on, I could see that Lila was becoming agitated. Finally she stood up and said,

"Ian the world does not come to an end at 2012. There are Mayan glyphs at prominent ruins that have the dates well into the year 4000 AD. The world is not going to end. The earth is not going to blow up. There may be earth changes, but that does not necessarily signify total annihilation. The earth is going to go on, and humanity will still be here. We will live through whatever may happen."

Ian was taken aback, but he was still very polite. They talked for a bit longer and then Lila said that she needed to attend to her children. I am very glad that I went with Ian that day. Although I do not have the inclination to study the complexities of the Aztec and Mayan calendars, it was good to hear what she had to say.

We stayed at El Portal for a few more days. By the time we were ready to go, most of the day lords names and the descriptions had been changed. The meanings of the numbers had also been transformed. The new Mayan Calendar and Conversion Chart was ready to manifest.

WHEN WE RETURNED, MANY OF THE ASPECTS OF THE second Mayan Calendar and Conversion Codex were finalized. I still helped Ian with the lay out. We made some mock-ups of the new codex. We had to go through a few different layouts until the codex that is available today came into full manifestation. The first batch of the new codices was printed in Mexico.

As the winter holidays were approaching, Ian threw himself into his jewelry. He wanted to make a lot for the holiday season. He did make some beautiful jewelry during that time. He had all of his molds with him now. He decided to make copies of a bracelet that was very wide and took a lot of silver to produce. He said that it was the Mayan Creation Story. The bracelet was the story of the Hero Twins. The Mayans have a myth that the Hero Twins started the Mayan civilization by playing a game of handball with the Lords of the Underworld. The twins had to journey to the underworld to play the game. The Lord of the Underworld tricked the Hero Twins and had them beheaded. The head of one of the Hero Twins was left hanging from a tree. Shortly after the Hero Twins had been beheaded, the daughter of the Lord of the Underworld walked by the head of one of the dead Hero Twins. The head started talking to her. During the conversation, the skull hanging on the tree spit in her hand and she became pregnant. Her father, The Lord of the

Underworld, banished her to the upper world. She went to the surface of the Earth and gave birth to a new set of Hero Twins. These young men, who were descended from the First Father and First Mother of the upper world and the Lord of the Underworld, grew up to start the Mayan civilization.

Ian showed me the drawing of the bracelet that he had copied from a book. When it was finally done, it was the same as the picture in the book, only in silver. It bent around my wrist perfectly. I decided not to be coy or polite. For turning my home into a jewelry lab, I wanted that bracelet for Christmas.

I took a class in Aura Soma Color Therapy in Sedona in October of 1999, so I was gone for a week. It was a very emotional class for me. I cried through most of it. I released a lot of the pent up emotions that had been inside of me. It was healing to get a little space in the relationship.

When I had come back from my class after being away for a week, I found it fantastic that Ian missed me. I was very tired when I came home that evening. Yet Ian was determined to make love to me. He kept me up all night. That was to be the last exquisite night of lovemaking we were to have. We still made love, but never again like that.

One night in early December, we had planned to go to Phoenix for the evening. Ian was taking a bath when the phone rang. A man's deep, soft voice came through the phone. He wanted to talk to Ian. I gave Ian the phone while he was sitting in the bath. He was sitting in a bath that was filled with an Aura Soma bottle that I had given him. The color of the liquid was gold. In the Aura Soma practice, the color gold represents financial abundance. Ian finally hung up the phone and sat in the bath for a long time.

When he got out of the tub he explained the situation to me in a calm, deep voice. He said that the man who called was someone he had met while I was up in Sedona, in October, taking my class. He said that the man wanted to invest in his project. He offered Ian $20, 000. This meant that Ian could go to Mexico and print his new codices! The timing was divine.

I was visiting a friend in Phoenix on December 18, 1999 and had left the apartment overnight. Ian was not home that night either. I went to my friend's house in Phoenix to get a little female bonding and nurturing. When I awoke the next day, I felt that I had to return home quickly. My friend kept saying that I should stay and take a bath. I took the bath, but jumped out of it very shortly after getting in. I just felt that I had to get home.

When I got home, there was black smoke coming out of my apartment window. I saw my gold cat sitting on the windowsill, meowing weakly. I opened the door and got him outside immediately. I had to let the smoke clear out a bit, so that I could go in and find my grey cat. I found her in the closet and she was not breathing. When I got her outside into the fresh air she began to breathe again. If I had been ten minutes later, she probably would have died. Watching my cat come back to life was my Christmas present that year.

All the walls of the one bedroom apartment were black from the smoke. An overloaded outlet was at the apex of the fire. Nothing had been burned except this area near the outlet. Everything else was intact but covered with black soot. I found it incredible that in this apartment building that had eight apartments in it no one called 911. I had been told that the smoke had been coming out of the apartment for hours.

After I took the cats to the emergency room, a friend took all three of us to her house. Ian went to stay with a friend of his friend Millie. The cats and I stayed there three days and then another friend let me house sit her home, which was a big dome, while she went away for the holidays.

The cats were doing well in a few days. When I went back to start the arduous cleanup of the apartment, I found something incredible. Genny, my cat that had been affected the most by the fire, had done something extraordinary. I had pictures of the head of the Shroud of Turin in an envelope on one of the shelves that were built into the closet. Genny had pulled down the envelope with the pictures in it and walked on it (her black soot paw prints were all over the envelope). She then lay down next to the envelope that contained the pictures of the Shroud of Turin. She was lying next to the envelope, not breathing when I found her. When I made this discovery, I started to cry again. I felt that the energy of the picture had kept her alive and watched over her until I was able to rescue her.

I was still a nervous wreck. I had never felt this bad in my life. Ian had come back and gotten his belongings out of the blackened apartment. He felt the fire was a sign that our time together was over.

AFTER CHRISTMAS PASSED, I HEARD FROM IAN AGAIN. He wanted to come over and spend some time with me before he went to Cancun, Mexico. The night that he came over was supposed to be a powerful night. According to information on the Internet, the moon was coming very close to the earth and the sky would be very bright. The moonlight was the brightest that it would ever be in our lifetimes.

I opened the door wearing a sexy, black dress. The smile on his face and the gleam in his eyes told me that he did have feelings for me and he did still find me attractive. We made dinner and we made love for the last time.

Throughout the night we laughed, we cried, we kissed each other abundantly and held each other tightly. I slept in his arms. We both felt complete as we watched the sun rise together.

In the morning, before we said good-bye, Ian told me that he would be landing in Cancun, Mexico on December 31, 1999. He would be on Mexican soil to witness Y2K.

I knew that he was doing what he felt he needed to do, and so was I. It was time for me to reconstruct my life without him. I would move into a new home on January first, 2000 and start anew.

DURING THE TIME THAT IAN WAS IN CANCUN, WE kept in touch by email. For the first nine months of 2000, Ian got the second Mayan Calendar and Conversion Codex printed. He sold them to many stores in Cancun. He was also trying to make a deal with a large water park near Cancun. All of these projects in Cancun never really came to fruition. By the time Ian left in September of 2000, he was seeing his charts and codex reproduced in many stores.

During this time, Ian wanted me to sell the codices for him in the US, but I had to decline. I was still too wounded from all that had happened. I was still in love with him, and I knew it would be easier for me to get over him if I had no continual connection with him. Ian turned the sale of the codices over to a mutual friend.

Even though Ian's time in Cancun was very troubled and beset with disappointment, a great situation came out of that time period. It was in Cancun that Ian met Carl Calleman. The Swedish biologist had created some fascinating theories about the Long Count calendar of the Maya. Ian told me about him. Ian and Carl spent a couple of months together. It was during that time that Ian was able to get a first-hand understanding of Dr. Calleman's theories. Ian came back from Cancun with a new zest for the knowledge that could be gleaned from Dr. Calleman's interpretation of the Long Count Mayan calendar.

Our friend suggested to Ian that he start a lecturing career when he came back from Cancun. Ian was excited by the work of Dr. Calleman. Ian decided to become a full time lecturer, spreading Dr. Calleman's ideas. Ian had shifted gears and was being reborn, like the evening star of the Venus cycle in the legend of Quetzalcoatl. He had gone through a great purification process with Mayan astrology and was now reinventing himself as a lecturer. I was glad when I found out that he had brought into being a new calling. He was still interested in the Mayan astrology, but now he became swept up in spreading the exciting information that Dr. Calleman had discovered.

THE LAST TIME I SAW IAN WAS CHRISTMAS OF 2002, when we both showed up to the same party. I was happy to see him again. When I ran into him that last time, I saw the lightning bolts around his head, as I had the first time I had met him. That sight helped me realize that he did love me, and would probably always have feelings for me. I felt a glimmer of the old flame that had once burned between us.

When I saw the little lightning bolts around his head, I found it curious that I only saw them around half of his head. I realized later, that the side where there were no lightning bolts was the side of his head where a tumor had started to grow.

About a year later, Ian went to a dentist and was told to go to a doctor. It turned out that he had a large, malignant tumor next to his vocal cords. This started a two-year saga of misery as Ian tried one holistic remedy after another to treat the cancer.

During the last three weeks of Ian's life, I kept feeling very sad and depressed. Ian had left Canada and wanted to be in Mexico when he passed. I was feeling his emotional sorrow every day of those last three weeks. I did not want to feel traumatized, but it made me realize that I was still connected to him. Then, on the bright autumn day of November 16, 2005, the sadness was gone. I was calm and the anguish was over. I found out three days later that Ian had passed on the day that I had finally felt at peace.

Epilogue

Ian's Quest for Standardization of the Tzolkin

IN THE 13 YEARS SINCE IAN AND I MET, HIS CHARTS AND the Kiché Maya count of the Tzolkin have become the standard that most people now use to follow Mayan astrology. His artwork of the Mayan day lords have been used by many authors and can even be found online, a bit altered, in the Wikipedia encyclopedia. Even though he is not in the body to see his victory, his battle to bring the standardization of the count of the Tzolkin to the world has been won. He has made a great contribution to the field.

I feel that I finally know why I channeled that picture of him thirty years ago. One day, while we were living together, Ian turned to me, as he was sitting at the computer and said, "You need to devote yourself to my work" I, of course, was offended. I had my channeling that I wanted to pursue. Now I feel that I will be part of the movement to bring Mayan astrology to the attention of the general public.

I moved to Sedona, AZ six months after Ian did, in 2001, and started a spiritual and healing practice that includes channeling, psychic readings, spiritual medium work, Reiki energy healing, Past Life Regression, massage and Western and Mayan astrology. In 2009, I got another strong message that it was time to share the story of what Ian and I created together with the world.

It was Ian's dream, when we were together, that the people of the Earth learn to be in harmony with the frequencies that come from the center of our galaxy by following the True Count of the Tzolkin.

It is my hope that this book will stimulate interest in what Ian created: his method of accessing and implementing the astrology of the Maya.

To get the Mayan Calendar and Conversion Codex go to:

www.SpiritualGuidance.Com

Or

www.MayanMajix.com

About the Author

ABBY ISADORA HAYDON HAD HER FIRST PSYCHIC experience at age eight when she saw her little brother's astral body standing next to his physical body, as he slept with his mother. Her little brother's astral body was laughing at her as she ran back to her room, closed the door and turned on all the lights.

Her spiritual gifts began to fully emerge when she was going to college in Mexico in the early 1970's. It was there that she received her first deck of tarot cards. It was also in Mexico that her long association with the beings she channels, The Assembly of Light, began. As Abby's interest in spiritual healing modalities increased, so did her list of skills she has mastered.

Now, in addition to psychic readings and channeling, Abby also offers sessions in Past Life Regression, Western and Mayan astrology, Reiki energy healing, Integrated Energy Therapy and sound healing. Abby has been in Sedona, Arizona using her gifts to help others heal body, mind and spirit.

Abby is available for individual consultations in person or on the phone, groups, workshops and lectures. She can be reached via her website www.mayanastrologer.com.

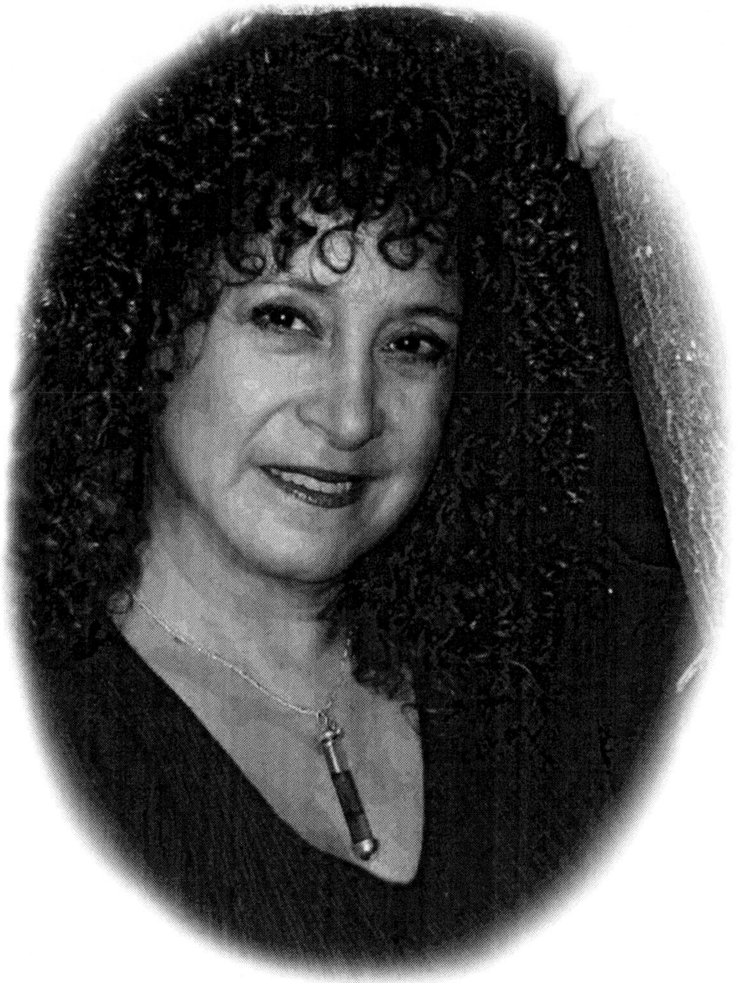